WO/MEN,
SCRIPTURE,
AND POLITICS

WO/MEN, SCRIPTURE, AND POLITICS

Exploring the Cultural Imprint of the Bible

ELISABETH SCHÜSSLER FIORENZA

 CASCADE *Books* · Eugene, Oregon

WO/MEN, SCRIPTURE, AND POLITICS
Exploring the Cultural Imprint of the Bible

Cascade Books
An Imprint of Wipf and Stock Publishers
199 W. 8th Ave., Suite 3
Eugene, OR 97401

www.wipfandstock.com

PAPERBACK ISBN: 978-1-4982-3532-7
HARDCOVER ISBN: 978-1-4982-3534-1
EBOOK ISBN: 978-1-4982-3533-4

Cataloguing-in-Publication data:

Names: Schüssler Fiorenza, Elisabeth, author.

Title: Wo/men, scripture, and politics : exploring the cultural imprint of the bible / by Elisabeth Schüssler Fiorenza.

Description: Eugene, OR: Cascade Books, 2021 | Includes bibliographical references and index.

Identifiers: ISBN 978-1-4982-3532-7 (paperback) | ISBN 978-1-4982-3534-1 (hardcover) | ISBN 978-1-4982-3533-4 (ebook)

Subjects: LCSH: Women—political activity. | Women in the Bible. | Bible—Influence. | Bible—Feminist criticism | Hermeneutics—Religious aspects.

Classification: BS538.7 S38 2021 (paperback) | BS538.7 (ebook)

08/20/21

For
Ziva Lev

Write the vision down . . .
For there is still a vision
For its own appointed time
Eager for its fulfillment

[Habakkuk 2:2–3]

CONTENTS

INTRODUCTION

WO/MEN,[1] *SCRIPTURE, AND POLITICS* was conceived and written during the time space marked by two presidential election campaigns, one in 2016 and the other in 2020. In the year the last state, Virginia, approved the Equal Rights (for wo/men) Amendment to the constitution, the *New York Times* endorsed two wo/men senators and presidential candidates, Elizabeth Warren and Amy Klobuchar.[2] However, neither candidate garnered enough support to be nominated by their party and therefore decided to end their campaigns. The eventual selection of Kamala Harris as vice-president confirms the cultural-biblical feminine stereotype, that woman is the "helpmate" of man based on the creation story in Genesis chapter 2. There are many

1. I write wo/men as well as s/he and fe/male in this way in order to indicate that the feminine form of grammar is inclusive of men and to indicate that gender labels are socio-politically constructed rather than given or natural. I am using the * to indicate that G*d in Greek the*s is neither masculine or feminine but unfathomable and undefinable, in place of the Greek roots *theos* or *thea,* which indicated masculine or feminine gender.

2. New York Times Editorial Team, "Democrats' Best Choice for President."

reasons for this failure of the democratic cultural-political imagination. One of them is, I suggest, that we do not have a cultural biblical imprint or code for women's presidency.

In this book, I seek to articulate and use biblical interpretation as intervention into this problem. Such an intervention is politically necessary but a "no-no" for academic scholarship, which often still claims to be value neutral and apolitical. Yet political analysis and interpretation of the Bible is called for because political argument utilizes biblical rhetoric in the public square.

The democratic understanding of the presidency has been jeopardized by the use of the Bible to legitimize the autocratic behavior of President Trump. For instance, conservatives have associated him with King Cyrus II despite the fact that the American president is not supposed to be a king. This book attempts, therefore, to intervene in the US cultural-political discourse on the "Bible in the Public Square."[3] The immediate socio-political location of this work is the 2016 US presidential election and the ensuing Constitutional crisis not only of the presidency but also of leading democratic institutions. However, the reach of this crisis is not restricted to the United States; it is global. This democratic crisis is of worldwide dimensions, not only because of the global neoliberal influence of the US but also because of its context of global poverty, migration, and climate deterioration.

Such an explicitly political introductory announcement of a book on the Bible's socio-political location and standpoint goes against all injunctions to practice scientific

---

3. See Barber, *Third Reconstruction*; Berlinerblau, *Thumpin' It*; Werline and Flannery, *Bible in Political Debate*; Briggs et al., *Bible in the Public Square*; Callahan, *Talking Book*; Chancey et al., *Bible in the Public Square*. Coote, *Power, Politics, and the Making of the Bible;* Scholz, *Biblical Studies Alternatively*; Scholz, *Bible as Political Artifact.*

detachment and scholarly neutrality. However, such injunctions are outdated at a time when very sophisticated scholarship, knowledge, and technology are used to manage and
manipulate the democratic election process. Liberation
the*logians and critical scientists around the world have
stressed that knowledge is political because it is produced
within certain political situations and serves political interests. These thinkers have taught us the common-sense
wisdom of "what we see depends on where we stand."
Therefore, authors and journalists can no longer pretend
that their standpoint is value neutral and apolitical. Rather,
we owe it to our readers to articulate the "standpoint" and
"point of view" that shapes our work. We can no longer
pretend that we are supra-terrestrial, detached, value-
neutral beings who float in academic clouds and have no
standpoint on planet earth. Our horizon and knowledge are
determined by where we as scholars and authors "stand."

My theoretical entry point into this book's discussion
of wo/men and Scripture in the public square is, on the one
hand, that of a biblical scholar trained in historical-cultur-
al-religious criticism and, on the other, that of a feminist[4]
the*logian[5] whose work has critically explored the theoretical impact of kyriarchal[6] structures of domination in
the interest of wo/men who are the majority of the poor in
this world. Such explicit reflection on social and theoretical
location does not make us less objective. Rather, it makes us
more objective when we critically and theoretically explore

4. I understand feminism as "the radical notion that wo/men
are people," a definition developed by activist and scholar Cheris
Kramerae.

5. See note 2. The*logy is speaking about G*d, derived from the
Greek word *theos* or *thea* (masculine or feminine) and *legein* = to
speak.

6. See the introduction in Schüssler Fiorenza and Nasrallah,
Prejudice and Christian Beginnings, 1–26.

3

biblical texts and their imprint on society and culture. Such a biblical-reflective approach is especially necessary in the US, which was self-consciously founded on biblical principles as well as in Europe since the Bible has shaped Western history and culture.

THE 2016 ELECTION: USE OF THE BIBLE BY THE RELIGIOUS RIGHT

Hillary Rodham Clinton was the first woman in the history of the American Republic to be elected as president by the American people but not by the electoral college. Since the electoral college[7] vote still decides the US election, although it is politically long outdated, Donald J. Trump and not Hillary Rodham Clinton occupied the presidency in 2016. To cover up that Clinton and not he was elected president by a wide margin of the popular vote, he continued his vindictive campaign chant "Lock her up!" at his rallies. Trump's presidency was in question from its very beginning as the gerrymandering of the electoral process and Russian electoral intervention in support of his campaign placed a stamp of illegitimacy on his presidency.Despite these crimes, he kept the presidency because of Republicans sabotaging and refusing to indict him in the Senate's impeachment trial.

Insofar as Trump's election was supported by the Religious Right, a biblical justification of his presidency continues to be necessary. His legitimacy was in question from the very beginning since he was elected only by a small majority of the electoral college. Evangelicals found such

7. West, "It's Time to Abolish the Electoral College." Darrell M. West is vice president and director of Governance Studies and holds the Douglas Dillon Chair. He is founding director of the Center for Technology Innovation at Brookings and editor-in-chief of TechTank.

a legitimization in the person of the Persian pagan King Cyrus mentioned in the Bible (Isa 45), who was described as a "Messiah" even though he did not follow the God or laws of the Israelite people. This choice of a biblical figure for Trump's religious legitimization has the political advantage that as a figuration of the biblical King Cyrus, Trump does not need to live and govern according to biblical values but is still authorized by the Bible. It is therefore necessary to look critically both at the biblical legitimization of Trump's presidency as King Cyrus, and also at the Bible and its availability for use by the political propaganda machine to fight against and demean a Democratic rival, especially a woman rival, competing for the presidency.Since Kamala Harris was selected by Biden as vice-presidential running mate, we also need to be aware how easily the Bible can be used against a wo/man in the vice presidential subordinate role. While we celebrate this historic choice of a woman vice-president, we also need to be aware that her poltical influence could be easily circumscribed by the use of the biblical-cultural stereotype, that "woman is the helpmate of man."

RAPAILLE'S "CULTURAL IMPRINT" AND BIBLICAL-POLITICAL ANALYSIS

In this book I also seek to explore different critical approaches to public biblical discourse, including the work of marketing theorist and anthropologist Clotaire Rapaille. While Rapaille's reliance on "reptile brain" theory is questionable, his theory and explication of the concept of "cultural imprint" used in marketing theory seems significant for biblical-political studies even though this theory has, as far as I know, not yet been developed and tested in the field. Rapaille argues that "the combination of the

experience and its accompanying emotion relates to something known widely as an imprint . . . Each imprint makes
us more of who we are. The combination of imprints defines
us."[8] Imprints differ from culture to culture. Hence, every
imprint influences us at an unconscious level in different
ways shaped by culture, and as a result cultural codes differ
based on culture. For instance, I have always been shocked
that Americans would call a woman senator or presidential
candidate "Madame," because in my German perception it
is a degrading title. However, this emotional reaction overlooked the difference in cultural code. In American Eng-
lish, the word "Madame" has two different meanings: it can
mean a woman of refinement or a woman who runs a house
of prostitution. In German, "Madame" has only one meaning. It refers to a woman who is running a brothel where
prostitutes work for money.

Since "cultural imprinting" analysis is not only used for
advertising beer or cars, but also in presidential campaigns,
critical biblical scholarship needs to analyze the cultural-
political imprints of the Bible in the public-political sphere.
People in traditionally Christian cultures carry cultural
biblical imprints that are often unconscious but influence
our values, beliefs, and perceptions of what is appropriate
or inappropriate to do or think.

According to Rapaille, the American cultural imprint
of the presidency was shaped by the revolution. Americans,
he argues, do not want a father figure as president, but a
leader with a strong vision "who makes us pay attention."
They want "a rebellious leader with a strong vision and the
will to get them out of trouble."[9] According to Rapaille, the
cultural code for the American presidency is Moses and the
American culture code is "dream." "We are the product of

8. Rapaille, *Culture Code*, 6.

9. Rapaille, *Culture Code,* 180.

6

dreams and we are the makers of dreams."[10] This conclusion points to the drastic change of the political-biblical-cultural code that imagines Trump as King Cyrus. It is no longer Moses who calls us to leave the bondage of Egypt, but a foreign King-Leader who compels us to adjust to bondage.

Rapaille argues that Americans want as president someone with a strong "reptilian brain" who can take care of our country. We want someone who can help us rebel against our problems and lead us into the promised land, because he knows what is wrong and how to fix it. We don't want a father figure. We want a biblical figure. Thus, for Rapaille, the figure of Moses emerges as the "culture code" for the American presidency.[11] He arrives at this conclusion by interviewing people about their earliest memories of the president and reviewing American history and the concept of the culture code, which includes biblical elements. While his argument that it is not Jesus but Moses who represents the code for the American presidency is interesting,[12] it should give us pause that it is not Moses but Cyrus II (600–535 BCE), known as Cyrus the Great, King of Persia[13] who has been used as the explicit culture code for Trump's presidency. This was overlooked by the Democrats in Trump's impeachment trial, as the appeal to a president's responsibility for the care for his people that the founders enshrined in the constitution has fallen on deaf

---

10. Rapaille, *Culture Code,* 195.

11. Rapaille, *Culture Code,* 186.

12. Rapaille, *Culture Code,* 186.

13. See for instance, Burton, "Biblical Story the Christian Right Uses to Defend Trump"; Dabashi, "Is Trump a King Cyrus or Queen Esther"; Moss, "Biblical Sites, Ancient Wonders, the Last 'Garden of Eden'"; de la Rosa, *Trump the US King Cyrus and the American Prayer*; "Chaos Candidate"; Ophoff, "Debunking the Trump-Cyrus Prophecy."

ears, because another biblical imprint has been fostered and is at work in Trump's popular appeal.

TRUMP AS "KING CYRUS II" IN FUNDAMENTALIST POLITICAL RHETORIC

At his visit in March 2018 president Netanyahu of Israel likened the president to King Cyrus:

> We remember the proclamation of the great King Cyrus the Great Persian King. Twenty-five hundred years ago, he proclaimed that Jewish Exiles in Babylon can come back and rebuild our temple in Jerusalem . . . And we remember how a few weeks ago, president Donald J. Trump recognized Jerusalem as Israel's capital. Mr. President, this will be remembered by our people throughout the ages.[14]

Identifying Trump with the pagan King Cyrus the Great enables right-wing politics that are biblically-based and allows for overlooking all the president's biblical offenses against the democratic care for the people. It is often pointed out and puzzled over in the press why the imprint of King Cyrus II is so persuasive for Trump's white evangelical followers, since the king was not a believer and did not worship the G*d of Israel. This puzzlement overlooks the biblical motif of "chosenness": Cyrus II is chosen by G*d for saving G*d's elect people, Israel. This reference to and legitimization of the biblical pagan King Cyrus functions as a cultural imprint which allows and enables fundamentalist acceptance of Trump as a presidential leader.

This the*logical framing is overlooked by liberals overall as well as journalists, politicians, and scholars in

---

14. Burton, "Biblical Story the Christian Right Uses to Defend Trump."

particular who bemoan the fact that Christian fundamentalism supports Trump's political actions, especially his racist prejudice and harsh politics against asylum seekers and immigrants, which goes against all biblical ethos. It does not help to quote the great commandment or the Sermon on the Mount, for example, to critique Trump's cruel actions on the southern border since his cultural scriptural imprint is that of King Cyrus the Great, who as a "pagan" ruler is not bound by biblical commandments and ethos. According to this cultural scriptural imprint, the president is not to be evaluated according to democratic Christian or Jewish presidential cultural and religious criteria, but as a "pagan" king who can act as such outside democratic controls and biblical ideals. This assumption has also been at work in the Republican Senate rebuttal of Trump's impeachment by the House.

While fundamentalist commentators are free to engage in the practice of literalist interpretation and to authorize right-wing politics with biblical prooftexts or appeals to biblical imagination, progressive politics with its roots in Post-Enlightenment critical thinking and scientific analysis has no such easy access to the apolitical use of the Bible. In consequence, biblical scholarship has not developed arguments and theoretical frames for engaging in a critical use of the Bible for political ends. True, liberation the*logy has gained some foothold in the academy during the eighties and nineties of the last century, but it has not developed critical methods and ways to interpret the Bible in the public square today. Political biblical exegesis and interpretation has not yet been sufficiently developed in the academy or by democratic think-tanks to be used for political argument in the public square. Considering the paradigms of interpretation at work in biblical studies might be helpful here.

REFRAMING BIBLICAL-POLITICAL
CULTURAL CODES

The Four Paradigms of Biblical Interpretation

In my work, I have outlined four paradigms of biblical interpretation: the traditional canonical paradigm of the church
fathers and rabbis; the scientific-historical paradigm of the
Enlightenment academy; the literary-cultural paradigm
that emerged in the 1970s; and the political-rhetorical paradigm of liberation and political the*logies of all stripes.[15]

The Christian "Patristic" and medieval interpretations of the traditional-canonical paradigm identified the
following four-senses of scriptural meaning: the *literal*
meaning of the text; the *allegorical* interpretation according
to which the meaning of Scripture pertains to the church;
the *eschatological* meaning in turn relates to heaven; and
finally the *tropological* meaning which refers to the moral
senses of Scripture. Similarly, rabbinic scriptural interpretation, which the rabbis call PaRDeS (Paradisical Garden),
has four levels of meaning. *Peshat* refers to the plain sense
of the Tanakh; *Remez* articulates its implied or allegorical
sense, while *Derush* entails legal and narrative exegesis and
Sod seeks for the mystical sense inscribed in the text. Early
Christian, so-called Patristic, and Jewish rabbinic interpretations of Scripture can be summarized in the following
Medieval jingle designed to be easily remembered:

> The **literal** teaches what G*d and our ancestors
> did, the **allegory** is where our faith and belief is
> hid, the **moral** meaning gives us the rule of daily
> life and the **anagogy** shows us where we end our
> strife.[16]

15. See the discussion of paradigms in my book, *Democratizing
Biblical Studies*, 51–84.

16. See Tracy and Grant, *Short History of Biblical Interpretation*.

This framework is also influential for modern evangelical interpretations of the Bible.

Modern scientific biblical interpretation, located primarily in the academy, has developed three different paradigms of interpretation: the historical-critical paradigm to replace the traditional canonical paradigm and the literary-cultural paradigm that abandons the historical search for sources and reads the Bible as a literary and cultural text whose interpretation depends on its cultural contexts, ideological developments, and biblical readers. Emerging from literary criticism, reader-response criticism in turn has opened the door for liberation the*logical and diverse political analyses of biblical texts.[17] While liberation the*logical readings often remain tethered to the*logical interpretation, reader-response criticism opened the door for culture-critical and critical feminist, postcolonial, and other political readings which enabled the emergence of the fourth paradigm of interpretation: political-rhetorical paradigm of liberation. Rapaille's suggestion of cultural code analysis might be helpful here.

However, if in Rapaille's view Moses is the cultural code for the American presidency, where does this leave women who are competing for the presidency? Are they to become like Moses chastising and punishing wo/men who, like Miryam in Numbers 12, challenge the status quo? Will the biblical imprint of Miryam's story and figure make it culturally very difficult to displace Moses, the national code figure of the American presidency? Does the American presidential code require that a woman candidate be punished like Miryam as the chant "Lock her up!" at Trump's rallies

17. For development of reader-response criticism outside of biblical studies, see Iser, *Act of Reading.* Such literary methods have been applied to a range of biblical texts. See for instance, Fowler, *Let the Reader Understand.*

still require from his ardent followers. Will the culturally inscribed biblical figures or images of the "Mary = Mother/ Miryam = Sister/Magdalene = Madam" (keeper of a whore house), inscriptions that are culturally pre-conscious, again torpedo the election of a woman as president? Can a wo/man according to such marketing theory and praxis ever fill the shoes of Moses or of King Cyrus the Great?

How can we find a biblical figure to refashion the political culture code for presidential wo/men candidates to replace the central biblical male code? To do so, we would need not only to trace the cultural imprints that emotionally allow us to desire a woman president, but also to critically choose a central biblical figure who could provide a biblical cultural code for the presidency of wo/men. This search for a biblical woman figure would require that marketing strategies and presidential campaign advisors become knowledgeable about biblical iconography and imagination. They need to encourage biblical studies to develop research on the biblical culture code, i.e., "the unconscious meaning we apply to any given thing. . . via the culture in which we are raised."[18] They also need to develop an analytic of biblical texts and their imaginative emotional imprints in light of public political interests. This would mean that biblical studies become also critical political studies. A biblical figure who comes to mind is Deborah. She could function as such a biblical figure and code for the presidency of a wo/man, because she has inspired the struggle for her nation's well-being.

18. Rapaille, *Culture Code,* 5.

Introduction

Deborah as Cultural Code for Woman President

Deborah, I suggest, is such a Moses-like scriptural woman figure. The story of Deborah[19] is found in Judges 4:4–24. Deborah is a woman prophet. She is characterized as a "lappidot-woman" (4:4, NRSV), a characterization that is often rendered in translation as "wife of Lappidoth," but actually means "woman of torches."[20] As "torch-woman" she is judge and political leader of Israel at the same time in Israel's pre-monarchy time. Deborah summons the warrior Barak and in the name of JHWH commands him to gather an army for fighting against Sisera, the head of Yabin's opposing army. Barak respond to Deborah's call saying: "if you go with me, I will go." The song celebrating their victory over King Yabin of Canaan is found in chapter 5 of the book of Judges.

The song of Deborah is a hymn of praise and at the same time tells the story of the battle for Israel's liberation from the occupation of Sisera. It begins at the time when all trade in Israel ceased and there was no peace in Israel. There was no deliverance until Deborah as leader and prophet arose. She is named "mother in Israel"and called by the people to enlist the warrior Barak.

In short, I have pointed to the story of Deborah, in order to identify a biblical figure who could function as a biblical icon for a woman president. To elect a woman as president of the US, it is important that we recognize a cultural biblical imprint that would inspire trust, respect, and enthusiasm for women candidates, because American

19. For a short summary see Kenski, "Deborah"; for extensive discussion see Jost, *Frauenmacht und Männerliebe*; Fewell, "Judges," 75f.

20. In Mesopotamian mythology the torch and lightning are heralding the storm God. The characterization of Deborah as "woman of torches" or "fiery woman" underscores her ability to rule justly.

13

culture and politics has been shaped by the Bible.[21] To adopt and identify with the biblical cultural imprint of Deborah is important because her scriptural image of "mother of the people," as judge and commander in chief, needs to be recognized and adopted by democratic political campaigns as important for legitimizing a woman candidate. It is important to replace in the cultural and religious imagination the image of Trump as biblical pagan King Cyrus with a woman candidate who is like Deborah, "mother of the people." While the Republican presidential campaign often heartily works with biblical image and language, the Democratic campaign still needs to address the biblical-religious cultural imprint of the image of the president as "commander in chief" and how this cultural imprint can be associated with a woman in the democratic imagination of the American presidency. This is necessary to replace the presidential warrior imprint of King Cyrus in the American cultural imagination. I suggest that the biblical image of Deborah as "mother of the people," who is already, I would argue, represented by Speaker of the House Pelosi, could provide a presidential imprint for electing a woman president.

Although women are now full members of the military, the "commander in chief" imprint is still male and masculine, since there are no historical examples of wo/men presidents. The founding history of the United States has rejected the cultural imprint of monarchy with its long history of queens as heads of state and replaced the monarchy with a rotating electoral democratic presidency that has been traditionally defined by the male/masculine image of the president as commander-in-chief. Hence, it is important to identify cultural biblical imprints of women

21. Hanson, *Political History of the Bible in America*; Harris-Lacewell, *Barbershops, Bibles, and BET*; Held Evans, *Inspired*; Hill Fletcher, *Sin of White Supremacy*; Jefferson, *Jefferson Bible*.

as heads of state. I have argued here that the biblical figure of Deborah as "national mother" defending the nation in war and peace should receive serious consideration in political discourse. In contrast to the mother of Sisera who is focused on her son, Deborah as mother of the nation is willing to accompany Barak and his army into battle for the benefit of her people. If Moses is the cultural imprint for the American male presidency, then we need to search for a different cultural biblical imprint for the presidency of wo/men. I have suggested here, that the cultural Scriptural imprint of Deborah as the mother of the nation could open up the American cultural-political imagination for a women president.

OUTLINE OF THE BOOK

The biblical-political analysis and suggestions of this book are developed in four chapters focusing on the role of the Bible in struggles over women's leadership in the present. The first chapter works with a feminist "double bind" analysis, which has been developed by Deborah Tannen, a feminist scholar of linguistics. This chapter argues that the ideological double bind which makes being a "good" woman and an effective leader mutually exclusive is rooted in biblical mandates for women's subordination encoded in the "household code" tradition. Chapter 2 discusses and engages a womanist the*logical analysis of the biblical Sarah-Hagar story, whereas chapter 3 focuses on the literary analysis and political deployment of the Jezebel story and character. The fourth and last chapter looks at the #MeToo movement and uses again Clotaire Rapaille's work on "cultural imprint" and "culture code." It seeks to understand how the stories of the three biblical Miryams/Marys speak to the cultural sphere of the feminist #MeToo movement.

The chapters of the book can be read in sequence but do not need to be read in such a way. They also can be read in terms of topic and focus. I hope readers will add their own biblical examples that inspire them to struggle for a biblical vision of "women in the public square."

1

THE BIBLE AND THE
CULTURAL "DOUBLE BIND"

DURING THE 2016 PRESIDENTIAL campaign Deborah Tannen, a feminist scholar of linguistics, pointed in a number of
articles to the "double bind" that makes a woman presidential candidate like Hillary Clinton appear inauthentic and
not trustworthy.[1] This "double bind" affects every progressive woman who competes for public office who clearly signals that she is not a subordinate of men. To quote Tannen:

> A double bind means you must obey two
> commands, but anything you do to fulfill one
> violates the other. While the requirements of a
> good leader and a good man are similar, the re-
> quirements of a good leader and a good woman
> are mutually exclusive . . . As Robin Lakoff, the

1. For a bibliography of her articles on the subject, visit https://
Deborahtannen.com/general-audience-articles/.

linguist who first wrote about the double bind confronting women, put it, male candidates can have it both ways but women candidates can have it no ways . . .The most difficult aspect of the double bind is that it is invisible; we think we are just reacting to the candidates as individuals. Yet, even the words to talk about women are drenched in gender.[2]

However, I would want to qualify this statement somewhat and argue that it applies almost exclusively to progressive women, while conservative wo/men candidates are exempt because they already have proven themselves to be "good women." Since a major cultural source of this double bind is the Bible, we need a hermeneutical lens that can detect this cultural double bind promulgated by Scripture and make this cultural inscription conscious. Biblical scholarship has the task to focus on the power relations of subordination inscribed in Scripture not just because of religious but also because of public-political reasons. In this chapter, I want to explore how Christian Scriptures continue to influence our public discourse and debates. Especially in crucial election seasons, it is important to recognize how Scriptural rhetoric and biblical ethos still shape American political discourses, public imaginations, and wo/men's recognition.

The debates around the appointment of Judge Kavanaugh to the Supreme Court, Dr. Blasey Ford's powerful testimony, and the courageous voices of the me-too movement that were drowned out by the high Republican approval ratings for this appointment have not been based on Scriptural references but nevertheless have been informed by the Scriptural ethos transmitted by these texts not so much concerned with the sexual abuse aspect of this debate

2. Tannen, "Self-Fulfilling Prophecy of Disliking Hillary Clinton."

but with the question of wo/men's and subordinate people's authority and power. I want to point out that despite the high approval of Senator Susan Collins who played the "good girl" or acted as the proper "white lady," the disrespect of wo/men in authority that played out at the Senate hearings has received little attention.

In contrast to Senator Collins's statement, North Dakota Senator Heidi Heitkamp's decision to vote against Brett Kavanaugh's Supreme Court confirmation cost her reelection. Senator Heitkamp revealed her reasons for voting against the nominee in an interview with CNN. She made her decision after she witnessed Kavanaugh's exchange with Minnesota's Senator Amy Klobuchar. The crucial point for her was how he behaved during his exchange with Senator Klobuchar, who asked Kavanaugh if he'd ever blacked out from too much drinking, to which he responded by asking her back, "Have you?" This was the decisive moment for Senator Heitkamp. She concluded that Kavanaugh did not have the demeanor for a Supreme Court Justice because he did not recognize Senator Klobuchar's standing and authority. He could not recognize a wo/man as his superior but reacted by trying to put himself on a level superior to her. This incident drove home that wo/men in positions of authority are still not respected and recognized, but instead are belittled and put in their feminine subordinate place![3]

This cultural lack of respect for wo/men in authority has deep roots in the Bible. We might remember 1 Tim 2:11–12: "Let a woman learn in silence with full submission. I permit no woman to teach or to have authority over a man, she is to keep silent!" Since the Bible is understood either as the "word of G*d" or as a revered cultural classic, it still undergirds Western cultural values and can be used

3. https://www.cnn.com/2018/10/08/politics/heidi-heitkamp-kavanaugh-cnn-interview/index.html.

in the interest of cultural and political domination. Hence, it is important to evaluate how this biblical cultural subconscious still shapes public discourses and political decisions. Bringing notions of Scripture and politics together can have an irritating, upsetting, and disturbing effect and jar religious imagination and sensibilities. Moreover, insofar as Scripture is also claimed to be the liberating word of a just and loving G*d, this rhetoric of justice stands in contradiction to and is incongruent with a scriptural rhetoric that advocates domination and submission.

Both the imperial language of domination with its violence and the democratic language of respect and love are encoded in Christian Scriptures and have shaped not only religious but also cultural self-understandings and ethos throughout the centuries and still do so today. The language of wo/men's subordination and control is not just a language from a forgotten historical past. Rather as language of Scripture it is performative language that still determines not only Christian but also American identity and praxis. It also has determined the refusal of Judge Kavanaugh to recognize a woman senator's authority.

This rhetoric does not need just to be understood but must also be made explicit and conscious. Since allusions to Christian ethos and Scriptures are still shaping public discourses today, this language of disrespect and domination of wo/men continues to be encoded in Western democratic political understandings, while the language of mutuality and community, which is also inscribed in the Bible, has become privatized as religious language restricted to the home and church.

This biblical rhetoric that denies wo/men's authority and calls for subordination is implicated in the economic-ecological impact of globalization and its attendant exploitation and misery. It has engendered the resurgence of the

Religious Far Right and of global cultural and religious fundamentalisms claiming the power to define the true nature and essence of religion.[4] Well-financed, right-wing think tanks are supported by reactionary political and financial institutions.[5] Moreover and most distressingly, right-wing religious movements around the globe have insisted in the past decades on the figuration of emancipated wo/men[6] either as signifiers of Western decadence and modern atheistic secularism, or they have presented "masculine" power as the expression of divine power. The interconnection between religious antidemocratic arguments and the debate with regard to wo/men's place and role in church, home, and society is not accidental. Nor is it merely a matter of intra-religious significance.

Tannen's notion of the "double bind" also explains Kavanaugh's behavior towards Senator Klobuchar. This "double bind" affects every progressive woman who competes for public office and thereby clearly signals that she is not a subordinate of men. In the biblical texts, we find a series of texts in the Christian Testament that have shaped and continue to shape American political imagination and discourse. This series of texts demands submission to the *kyrios,* a term that refers to the emperor as well as of the

4. See for instance the important study of Bendroth, *Fundamentalism and Gender* on fundamentalism in America as well as the variegated contributions in Küng and Moltmann, *Fundamentalism as an Ecumenical Challenge.*

5. For an excellent critical analysis of the involvement of religion in this global struggle see especially the work of the late Penny Lernoux, *Cry of the People*; Lernoux, *In Banks We Trust*, and her last book before her untimely death *People of God*; Reich, *Work of Nations*; Smith, "Creation of the World We Know," 27–41.

6. This writing of wo/men signifies that the expression wo/men is inclusive of men as well as that the power differences within wo/men and between wo/men can be greater than those between women and men of the same race, class, nation, culture or religion.

head of the household, the lord, slave master, and father—
that is, the elite propertied male. These texts are classified
as household codes, which is a label derived from Lutheran
teaching on social status and roles (*Ständelehre*).

Such household or domestic codes (*Haustafeln*) are
found in the so-called Deutero-Pauline, Pastoral, and Catholic Epistles (Col 3:18—4:1; Eph 5:21—6:9; 1 Tim 2:8–15;
5:1–2; 6:1–2; Titus 2:1—3:8; and 1 Pet 2:13—3:7). The basic
form of these household-code texts consists of three pairs
of exhortations addressing the relationship between freeborn wife and husband, children and parents, slaves and
masters. In each case, the socially subordinate first member
of the pair is exhorted to obedience and submission to the
superordinate second. In short, household code texts are
seemingly concerned with three sets of relationships: wife
and husband, slave and master and children and parents.
However, it must not be overlooked that in each case it is
the *kyrios*/father—the head of the household—to whom all
other the members of the household owe submission. The
central interest of these texts is to bolster the authority of
the *kyrios*, or in Latin the *paterfamilias*, by demanding submission and obedience from the socially weaker group—
wives, slave wo/men, children, and the whole community.

The earliest form of these so-called household codes
in the Christian Testament is found in the letter to the Colossians (Col 3:18—4:1) which reads:

> Wives, be subject to your husbands, as is fitting
> in the Lord. Husbands, love your wives and
> never treat them harshly. Children, obey your
> parents in everything, for this is your accept-
> able duty in the Lord. Fathers, do not provoke
> your children, or they may lose heart. Slaves,
> obey your earthly masters in everything, not
> only while being watched and in order to please

> them, but wholeheartedly, fearing the Lord. Whatever your task, put yourselves into it, as done for the Lord and not for your masters, since you know that from the Lord you will receive the inheritance as your reward; you serve the Lord Christ. For the wrongdoer will be paid back for whatever wrong has been done and there is no partiality. Masters, treat your slaves justly and fairly, for you know that you also have a Master in heaven.

This Christian Testament teaching on "male headship and female subordination" reflects the *oikos* or household ideal of the Roman Empire that calls for submission and subjection from members of the household, officers of the empire, citizens, vassals, and provinces.[7] It does not just affect elite married men and women and their relationships, but it calls for submission and subordination of all the subjects of the Roman empire, freeborn men and women, slave women and men, clients, and resident aliens. However, it must not be overlooked that these texts are not descriptive but prescriptive. They probably are responses to the egalitarian ethos of the *ekklēsia*, the democratic assemblies that met in houses (*oikoi*).[8]

7. Cf. Lassen, "Roman Family," 103–20; Martin, "Construction of the Ancient Family," 40–60; Rawson, *Marriage, Family and Divorce in Ancient Rome*; Rawson, "Children as Cultural Symbols."

8. See my book, *In Memory of Her*. Most recently Osiek and MacDonald, *Woman's Place* have revisited this argument with reference to the research of the last 25 years but without crediting my work. Rather they caricaturize the polarity patriarchy—discipleship of equals (note my alternative has been ekklesia—patriarchy/kyriarchy) and opt for the polarity honor-shame instead. While their other two assumptions—masculine titles do not just refer to men and women participated in all the activities of the house-church—also have been discussed at length in *In Memory of Her*, they do not refer to them or engage my theoretical reconstructive model.

Once again, it is important to bear in mind that these texts are not only concerned with three sets of household relationships: wife and husband, slave and master, and children and parents, but also with submission to the emperor. The central interest of these texts lies in enforcing patterns of submission and obedience[9] of socially weaker groups— the whole community, wives, slaves and children—on the one hand and in bolstering the authority of the head of household, the *paterfamilias* on the other. In the case of the emperor, this would have encompassed the whole empire.[10] To destabilize the kyriarchal household was then a threat to the order of the state.

This pattern of domination and subjection need not always include the four social status groups (freeborn male heads of household, slave wo/men, freeborn wives, and children) addressed in the epistle to the Colossians.[11] In other texts only some of the subordinate groups are mentioned. Most importantly, these are not just household codes but also imperial codes that demand obedience to the political powers of the Roman Empire. Such texts are used to ensure the ethos of submission not only for the household, but also for the Christian community, understood as a household of G*d, and its relation to society. Such injunctions to submissiveness occur already in the authentic Pauline letters,

9. The code is said to be completely incorporated in Col 3:18—4:1 and Eph 5:22—6:9. However, like in 1 Pet 2:18—3:7, it is not found completely in the remaining passages: 1 Tim 2:11,15; 5:3–8; 6:1–2; Titus 2:2–10; 3:1–2; 1 Clem. 21:6-8; Ign. *Pol.* 4:1—6:2; Pol. 4:2—6:1; Did. 4:9–11; Barn. 19:5–7. Hence, it would be better to call it the "code of submission" which can be used in various circumstances.

10. Syme, *Roman Revolution*, 509–24.

11. Cf. Nash, "Heuristic Haustafeln," 25–50. See also Standhartinger, "Origin and Intention of the Household Code in the Letter to the Colossians," 117–30.

for example, in Rom 13 and 1 Cor 14.[12] While this pattern of subordination functions differently in different early Christian documents and their social-ecclesial-historical contexts, the anti-democratic political pattern of submission seems to be characteristic for this ethos. This pattern of submission conceives not only of the family, but also of the state and the Christian community in terms of the kyriarchal household.

Familia in the Roman empire did not mean nuclear family; rather it encompassed all those who were under the authority of the *pater familias*, the father of the *familia*—wife, children, other relatives, and slaves. The household, *oikos* (Gk.) or *domus* (Lat.), included all those affiliated with it and included clients, day-workers, and even visitors.[13] The household in the Roman Empire was an economic production center, a central site of education and training in trade and craft skills, a guarantor of social services and the location of religious life.[14]

Politically, the household was a microcosm of the empire and the "nursery" of the state. As Cicero, a Roman philosopher and politician who lived in the first century BCE, so succinctly states:

> The first bond of union is that between husband and wife; the next that between parents and children; then we find one household with everything in common. And this is the foundation of civil government, the nursery (*seminarium*), as it were of the state. (*De Officiis* 17.54)

12. See Kittredge, *Community and Authority in Paul.*

13. Cf. Bradley, *Discovering the Roman Family*; Dixon, *Roman Family*; Cox, *Household Interests*; Gardner, *Family and Familia in Roman Law and Life*; Cohen, *Jewish Family in Antiquity*; Balch and Osiek, *Early Christian Families in Context.*

14. Cf. Barclay, "Family as the Bearer of Religion in Judaism and Early Christianity," 66–80.

The emperor was called *pater patrum*, the father of all fathers, and *pater patriae*, the father of the fatherland. The emperor was the ultimate father and lord (*kyrios*) par excellence. He was king of kings and lord of lords. According to Greco-Roman political ideology, a male citizen's authority rested in his dominance over his extended household.[15] Those elite male citizens who could not control their households risked losing control of the state. Hence, the emperor like any other elite male had to project and maintain a firm image of patriarchal control; he had to appear to be in full charge of his household in order to show that he was to be trusted as the ruler of the empire.

The letter to the Ephesians also contains a household code, and if one reads the household code in the letter to the Ephesians in this Roman political imperial context, the letter's highly political language comes to the fore. Not only is G*d the cosmic *pater familias* (Eph 3:14–15), the "father" (*pater*) from whom all father-power flows, but also Christ/Messiah takes the role and place of the emperor. The author elaborates the household in terms of the relationship between Christ and the *ekklēsia*. *Ekklēsia* is a feminine noun. While it is typically translated as "church" in most modern translations, the term *ekklēsia* might be better translated as "democratic decision-making assembly." The establishment of the Roman empire in Asia Minor brought the Greek democratic citizen government in the form of the *ekklēsia* into tension and conflict with the imperial political power of Rome. Read within this political frame, the author seems to favor imperial power over citizen power, when he argues

15. Saller, *Patriarchy, Property, and Death in the Roman Family*; Saller, "Women, Slaves, and the Economy of the Roman Household"; Saller, "Pater Familias, Mater Familias, and the Gendered Semantics of a Roman Household," 182–97; Saller, "Corporal Punishment, Authority, and Obedience in the Roman Household," 144–65.

that like the *ekklēsia*, freeborn wives, too, should be subordinate. However, such imperial kyriarchal power should be exercised in agape, love:

> Wives, be subject to your husbands as you are to the Lord.
>
> For the husband is the head of the wife just as Christ is the head of the church, the body of which he is the Savior.
>
> Just as the church is subject to Christ, so also wives ought to be, in everything, to their husbands. (5:22–24)[16]

CONTINUING INFLUENCE OF THE PATTERN OF SUBMISSION

Such Scriptural rhetoric of subordination still undergirds contemporary American politics and shapes the public of wo/men politicians. It is not accidental that the Christian Right and wide segments of the Republican party have made the family, sexuality, and the diminishment of the citizen rights of all wo/men, immigrants, black people, and the poor the central cornerstone of their political rhetoric.[17] The Bible is sometimes invoked but often implicitly fuels anti-democratic arguments, because it allegedly teaches the divinely-ordained subordination of all wo/men, migrants, and the creational differences between the sexes and races, as well as the abomination of homosexuality.

16. If you are interested to learn more about this text, please see my commentary on Ephesians in the feminist Wisdom Commentary series of Liturgical Press.

17. Cf. Radl, *Invisible Woman*; Diamond, *Spiritual Warfare*; Küng and Moltmann, *Fundamentalism as an Ecumenical Challenge*; "Fundamentalismen," ; Howland, *Religious Fundamentalisms and the Human Rights of Women*; Mason, *Killing for Life.*

This right-wing political rhetoric is so effective because it defends the nuclear American family in the name of biblical Christianity.

Susan Moller Okin, a feminist political philosopher, has shown some time ago that the classical political ideology of the biblical household codes still operates in contemporary American democratic society. Although household and family have been repeatedly modified in the course of history, contemporary political philosophy still accepts the premise of Greek and Roman classical philosophy which asserts that the free, propertied man is the full citizen, in relation to whom

> all the other members of the population—slaves and artisans as well as women—exist in order to perform their respective functions for the few free males who participate fully in citizenship. The "natures" of all these groups of people are defined in terms of their satisfactory performance of their conventional functions.[18]

In antiquity, the sphere of the household was important primarily as an economic base, whereas in modern times the nuclear family is crucial for affective life. Although liberalism is purportedly based on an individualism that understands society as constituted of "independent, autonomous units," it is clear, according to Moller Okin, that in spite of this individualistic rhetoric, the "nuclear patriarchal family" and not the adult human individual is the basic political unit of liberal and non-liberal political philosophy. The adult members of the family are assumed to share all the same interests. Yet, whenever a conflict of interest occurs between husband and wife, the presumption

18. Moller Okin, *Women in Western Political Thought,* 276.

in political and legal philosophy has been that a conflict of interest must be decided by the male head of household

Moreover, the public political sphere is defined by competition and self-interest, not by values of compassion, love, and altruism, since such values are relegated to the private sphere of the home as wo/men's, children's, and servants' domain. To legally and politically recognize wo/men as full citizens in their own right would entail, therefore, a change in both the family structure and in political philosophy and public discourse. Moller Okin concludes:

> If our aim is a truly democratic society, or a thoroughly democratic theory, we must acknowledge that anything but a democratic family with complete equality and mutual interdependence between the [adult members of the household] will be a severe impediment to this aim.[19]

In short, the Aristotelian political ethics of natural inequality has not only shaped the Bible but also Western political philosophy as well as society as a whole, and still does so. A truly democratic society would necessarily presuppose not only a radical transformation of the kyriarchal family, but also a radical transformation of our elite-male-centered civic society and politics. Although Moller Okin has recognized the historical and political philosophical interconnections between the state, civil society, and the family in antiquity and modernity, her analysis remains within the analytic framework of gender rather than reformulating it in terms of intersecting structures of domination.

Whereas "white" feminist theory has used as key analytic categories "woman, " "the feminine," "gender" (a grammatical-social construction), or "patriarchy" (the

---

19. Moller Okin, *Women in Western Political Thought,* 289. See also her book *Justice, Gender, and the Family*.

domination of men over women), and has attempted to distinguish between sex and gender,[20] such a dualistic approach has been seriously questioned by Two-Third World feminists, who point to the multiplicative structures of domination determining wo/men's lives.[21]

In order to theorize structures of domination in antiquity and the multiplicative intersections of gender, race, class, and ethnicity in modernity, I have sought to articulate a feminist heuristic model that is able to articulate the intersecting structures of race, gender, class, ethnicity, and imperialism.[22] Hence, I have argued that we replace the notion of patriarchy/patriarchalism with the neologism "kyriarchy" articulated as a key analytic concept.[23] Kyriarchal relations of domination are built on elite male property rights over wo/men and are marked by the intersection of gender, race, class, and imperial domination, as well as by dependency, subordination, and obedience or second-class citizenship.

Such a kyriocentric ideology and social-system of kyriarchy is characteristic not only of ancient but also of modern western societies. Kyriarchal relations of domination and subordination are explicitly articulated in Western political philosophy inspired by Greek democracy and

20. See Nagl-Docekal, *Feminist Philosophy*; Jeffries, *Feminine Feminists*; Dekoven, *Feminist Locations*; Walby, *Patriarchy at Work*. Shanley and Pateman, *Feminist Interpretations and Political Theory*; Bussman and Hof, *Geschlecherforschung/ Gender Studies in den Kultur und Sozialwissenschaften*.

21. See Bryson, *Feminist Debates* and especially Sandoval, *Methodology of the Oppressed*. For this discussion in feminist the*logy see, e.g., Aquino et al., *Reader in Latina Feminist Theology*; Armour, *Deconstruction, Feminist Theology and the Problem of Difference*.

22. For a discussion of Roman imperialism see Champion, *Roman Imperialism*.

23. For the development of this concept and bibliographic documentation see my books, *But She Said*; *Discipleship of Equals*; *Jesus: Miriam's Child, Sophia's Prophet*; *Sharing Her Word*; *WisdomWays*.

they are continued by Roman imperialism. They have been mediated through Christian scriptural-theological traditions such as the "household codes" and have decisively determined modern kyriarchal forms and ideologies of democracy.

Modern political philosophy continues to assume that propertied, educated, elite, white, Western man is defined by reason, self-determination, and full citizenship, whereas all his Others are characterized by emotion, service, and dependence. We wo/men are still often seen not as rational and responsible adult subjects but as emotional, helpless, and child-like.

To sum up my argument: I have suggested that a critical feminist method and hermeneutical process of biblical interpretation is best understood as a process of detoxifying the biblical inscriptions of subordination and the second-class citizenship of subordinate wo/men in our public consciousness. A detoxifying process of interpretation challenges us to become ethically sophisticated readers of religious Scriptures and we can do so by reflecting on our own socio-political locations and functions in global economic and political structures of domination. At the same time, a critical feminist reading empowers us to struggle for a more just democratic society and religion.

Such an interpretive process is not restricted to Christian canonical texts but can be and has been used successfully by scholars of other religious traditions. Moreover, it is not restricted to the biblical scholar as expert reader. Rather, it calls all of us to become transformative and engaged interpreters, be it the Bible or the daily news. In and through such a critical rhetorical process of interpretation and deliberation, biblical texts can be critically investigated and become sites of struggle and conscientization. This ability to scrutinize biblical texts also enables us to become critical readers of all popular media.

In the context of global exploitation and domination of today, we must reject the theological, scriptural claims of the ethics of submission because of its oppressive effects on the life of wo/men and other subordinated peoples. The words of Angelina Grimké are good place to end: "The doctrine of blind obedience and unqualified submission to any human power, whether civil or ecclesiastical, is the doctrine of despotism."[24] Commitment to the emancipatory struggles for democratic citizenship for everybody therefore demands that we engage the ethos and praxis of coequality in community to engender transformations of the kyriarchal inscriptions of domination and subordination in Christian Scriptures, theologies, and consciousness, if we are to contribute to a radical democratic egalitarian future of well-being for all of creation.

---

24 Grimké and Grimké, *On Slavery and Abolitionism*, 97.

2

SARAH, HAGAR, AND THEIR/ OUR CHILDREN

As SCRIPTURE TEXTS, BIBLICAL texts are religious te
Jews and Christians. However, biblical texts are als
sic texts of Western cultures. Their cultural impri
deeply embedded in the cultural landscapes of the glo
documents of ancient patriarchal and kyriarchal cult
they continue to preach not only justice and love but also
transmit heterosexism, racism, misogyny, anti-Semitism,
and classism today. We therefore must not only seek to
understand these texts in their cultural contexts, but also
analyze the cultural imprints of biblical texts on readers
today. Such cultural imprinting is furthered and deepened
through liturgical proclamation and legitimization of the
text as sacred. Without pointing out the cultural imprints
of the Bible, our proclamation of Scripture as holy neglects

and obfuscates that the Bible is not just a religious but also a cultural text that requires critical analysis.

THE STORIES ABOUT ABRAM/ABRAHAM, SARAI/ SARAH, AND HAGAR

The stories about Sarai/Sarah, Hagar, and Abram/Abraham, are told in Genesis and used by the apostle Paul in a dualistic way to pit two communities against one another. The story of Sarai and Abram[1] goes as follows: Abram and his wife Sarai have to leave their native land to follow G*d's promise (Gen 11–23). Abram obeys G*d's call to leave his homeland and shortly after arriving in Canaan, he leaves again for Egypt to avoid a famine. Because his spouse Sarai was very beautiful, he commands her to tell the Egyptians who "had a reputation in the Israelite mind for sexual impropriety"[2] ___e is his sister and not his wife, so that no one would ___ in order to be able to marry her. When they arrive ___t, the people praise Sarai's beauty and the pharaoh ___er into his harem. To thank Abram for giving him ___ter," the pharaoh paid him richly with male and fe- ___ervants as well as animals and other goods. When ___araoh takes Sarai as his wife, G*d sends plagues to ___sh him (12:17) and the pharaoh releases her. Abram thus "essentially sex-trafficked his wife and profited richly."[3]

The stories of Sarah, Hagar, and Abraham which focus on the heirs of Abraham are told in Gen 16–21. Because

1. The names of Sarai and Abram are changed to Sarah and Abraham in Gen 17.

2. Berlin and Brettler, *Jewish Study Bible*, 31f. "Although Abraham is sometimes chastised for passing his beautiful wife off as his sister, it is hard to see how Sarai (whose name becomes Sarah in ch. 17) would have fared better if he died."

3. Lamb, "David was a Rapist, Abraham was a Sex Trafficker." See also his book, *Prostitutes and Polygamists*.

Sarai is barren, she asks that her Egyptian slave Hagar (Gen 16:1–14 and 21:8–21), the second primary wife[4] of Abram, bear him a son who will be the heir, since Sarai is childless. According to the text, when Hagar becomes pregnant, she looks "with contempt at Sarai" (16:4), Sarai then complains to Abram and he tells her that Hagar is in Sarai's and not in his power and that she should deal with her. Sarai punishes Hagar severely, and in response Hagar flees into the wilderness where G*d's angel promises her that she will bear a son, whom she should call Ishmael. Hagar recognizes the Lord who spoke to her and says in wonder; "Have I really seen G*d and remained alive after seeing G*d?" (Gen 16:13) G*d also promises Abram that Sarai, his wife, whom he should call Sarah from now on, will bear him a son. But Abraham laughs and asks whether a man who is hundred years old and has a wife who is ninety years old can have a baby (Gen 17:15–17). When Sarah heard, that she in her advanced age, shall have a son, she also laughs, and when the Lord chides her, she denies it, because she is afraid (Gen 18:9–15).

Chapter 21 of Genesis continues the story of Sarah and Hagar, the Egyptian, and their two sons. The two sons of Abraham grow up and play with each other. However, when Sarah sees the son of Hagar playing with her son Isaac, she says to Abraham: "Cast out the slave woman with her son. He is not to inherit with my son Isaac!" (21:8–10). Abraham is very distressed but is told by G*d to do what Sarah tells him because Isaac is Abraham's offspring (21:11–14), his heir, and will be the founder of a great nation. Hence, Abraham sends Hagar and her son with some bread and water into the wilderness. When this sustenance is gone,

---

4. Abraham had three primary wives, Sarah, Hagar, and Keturah (Gen 25:1) and an unknown number of secondary wives called concubines. DeYoung et. al., *People's Bible*, 156, note to Gen 25:1–6. See also Gafney, "Hagar."

Hagar walks away from her child because she cannot stand "to look at his death." G*d intervenes again through an angel and Hagar is told to open her eyes and lift up the boy, because G*d will make of Ishmael a great nation. When Hagar opens her eyes, she sees a well of water, gives the boy a drink, and Ishmael is revived. G*d continues to be with him growing up in the wilderness of Paran and we are told, that "his mother got a wife for him from the land of Egypt," her native land (21:20–21). This tale of Sarah, Hagar, and their sons tells the story of the beginnings of two great religions: Judaism and Islam.

PAUL'S USE OF THE STORIES OF SARAH AND HAGAR

This Genesis tale is retold by the apostle Paul in the letter to the Galatians. In chapter 4, Paul allegorizes this story of Sarah, Hagar, and their sons from the book of Genesis. An allegory tells a story that can be interpreted to reveal a hidden meaning, typically a moral or political one. Hence, scholars analyze such an allegory in theological, literary, and historical-cultural terms to recoup the hidden meaning of the story. To quote the apostle Paul:

> For it is written that Abraham had two sons, one by a slave woman and the other by a free woman. One, the child of the slave, was born according to the flesh; the other, the child of the free woman, was born through the promise. Now this is an allegory: these women are two covenants. One woman, in fact is Hagar, from Mount Sinai, bearing children for slavery. Now Hagar is Mount Sinai in Arabia and corresponds to the present Jerusalem, for she is in slavery with her children. But the other woman corresponds to the Jerusalem above; she is free and she is our

> mother . . . But what does the Scripture say?
> 'Drive out the slave and her child; for the child
> of the slave will not share the inheritance with
> the child of the free woman.' So then, friends, we
> are children, not of the slave but the free woman.
> For freedom Christ has set us free.[5]

As allegorical interpretations, early Christian and Jewish interpretations of Scripture are different from modern ones. Traditionally, four levels of meaning were distinguished in pre-modern interpretation theory:

> The **literal** was defined as teaching what God
> and our ancestors did, the **allegory** is where our
> faith and belief is hid, the **moral** meaning gives
> us the rule of daily life and the **anagogy** shows
> us where we end our strife.[6]

Paul tells the story of the two women, Sarah and Hagar, and their male children as an allegory that is as figurations of freedom and slavery. At the end of the third chapter of Galatians, Paul refers to but changes a text scholars consider to be a baptismal formula:

> There is neither Jew or Greek, slave or free, male
> and female, but you are all one in Christ (Mes-
> siah) Jesus. (Gal 3:28)

Paul then sums up this chapter with the statement: "And if you belong to Christ, then you are Abraham's offspring, heirs according to the promise" (Gal 4:29).

At the end of chapter 4 Paul refers to the allegory of Abraham's two sons, one born according to the flesh, whereas the other, the child of the free woman, was born through the promise (Gal 4:23–24). The text explains this

5. Gal 4:21—5:1.

6. See Grant, *Short History of Biblical Interpretation*.

allegory as follows: Hagar "is mount Sinai bearing children for slavery," whereas Sarah "corresponds to the Jerusalem above," who "is free and she is our mother" (4:25–26). Paul's allegory creates a dualism between Sarah and Hagar: Sarah is the free Jerusalem above and Hagar is seen as the enslaved Jerusalem of Paul's day. This metaphorical dualism does not, however, signify an actual historical dualism between Jews and Christians, as the text is often wrongly interpreted. Paul, as a Jew, writing to Jewish messianic converts in Galatia, uses the allegory to pit communities against each other, those who practice circumcision and those who do not.

Obviously, this allegory has no longer any immediate cultural significance for readers today in a culture where male circumcision is widely practiced for health reasons.[7] The cultural imprint of this text in our contemporary American context has lost the context of debates on circumcision that were of critical importance to Paul. What then is the cultural imprint or stereotypic message that this biblical text inculcates today? What is the unconscious bias it conveys to those who encounter it? Although many people who are practicing Christians or live in a Christian-typed culture have never read or heard of this text, we can nevertheless assume that it is still operative in the cultural subconscious of people in Europe, North and South America, and New Zealand/Australia, continents that have been shaped by biblical traditions. People in traditionally Christian cultures carry cultural biblical imprints that are often unconscious but influence our values, beliefs, and perceptions of what is appropriate or inappropriate to do or think. Hence, this text continues to function today not so much as Holy Scripture but much more as a cultural imprint pitting people against

7. For the medical discussion, see "Report of the Task Force on Circumcision," 388–91.

each other in religious terms: the African-American slave descendants against their previous white Christian masters, Christians against Jews or Muslims, white wo/men against wo/men of color, and poor people of all races and cultural backgrounds against the 1 percent of the super rich.[8]

THE CULTURAL IMPRINT
OF THE SARAH-HAGAR STORY

The Pauline allegorical, dualistic metaphor of the two women, Sarah and Hagar representing freedom and slavery, has been racialized[9] in Western history in general and American history in particular and as such it has become deeply engraved in Euro-American self-understandings. It no longer is simply a literary religious allegory but has become not only a cultural imprint and ingrained bias in European, American, or Australian and New Zealand political identity, but it also has been naturalized in racial and cultural-religious terms. The mass killing at the Mother Emanuel church in Charleston, South Carolina, the slaughter of the congregants of the Tree of Life Jewish Synagogue in Pittsburgh, and the two mosques where Muslim worshipers were murdered in Christchurch, New Zealand, bespeak the mostly unconscious bloody cultural imprint of this text of Christian Scripture.

8. Trible and Russel, *Hagar, Sarah, and Their Children*. This excellent collection of essays edited by Phyllis Trible and Letty M. Russel explores the Sarah—Hagar traditions and their imprint in an US American context.

9. Merriam-Webster defines "racialization" as "act or process of imbuing a person with a consciousness of race distinctions or of giving a racial character to something or making it serve racist ends." *Merriam-Webster.com,* s.v. "racialization," https://www.merriam-webster.com/dictionary/racialization.

Anti-Judaism

Paul's text is traditionally interpreted in a binary fashion as pitting Christians against Jews, since Paul is generally understood to be a Christian and not a Jew. Recent research on Paul has, however, recovered Paul, the Jew, who was not a "Christian" in our sense of the word but a follower of the Jewish Messiah figure Jesus.[10] Recent research has tried to correct this misunderstanding but has generally not succeeded to change the understanding of Paul as a Christian in Western cultural contexts. Such a bias of Christian anti-Judaism was also active in the beginnings of the feminist movement in religion and in Christian feminist the*logy.[11] While Christian wo/men scholars did not invent Christian anti-Judaism, they often unwittingly reproduced it.

This anti-Jewish misunderstanding figured Sarah as the mother of Christians and Hagar as representing Judaism. Christian anti-Judaism and superiority claims in turn are the scriptural roots of the Holocaust and have most recently served as right-wing justification for the massacre of worshipers in the Tree of Life, *L'Simcha* Congregation in the Squirrel Hill neighborhood of Pittsburgh, Pennsylvania, on October 27, 2018, while Shabbat morning services were being held.[12]

White Racist Supremacy

However, Paul's binary of Sarah vs. Hagar has not only legitimized anti-Judaism but also white racist supremacy, since this binary pits the free woman Sarah and the enslaved

10. Boyarin, *Radical Jew*. See also Boyarin, *Jewish Gospels*.

11. See Schüssler Fiorenza, *Jesus and the Politics of Interpretation*, 115–44.

12. Robertson et al., "11 Killed in Synagogue Massacre; Suspect Charged With 29 Counts."

woman Hagar against each other. This text has been active in the context of the American history of slavery. The deadly shootout by a young white supremacist in the historic Mother Emmanuel Black church in Charleston, South Carolina on June 17, 2015 killed nine African-American congregants at prayer and Bible study.[13]

Biblical texts like the Sarah-Hagar allegory of Paul have engendered in the US a racial cultural imprint that pits Sarah, the mistress of the house, and Hagar, the sex-slave surrogate, against each other. African-American Womanists have theorized that Hagar the slave who was impregnated by her master and cast out into the desert is a symbol of the dehumanization that African slave wo/men and their offspring have suffered in America. Delores Williams has pointed out that two African American traditions of biblical interpretive appropriation exist: one is black liberation the*logy, which has been developed primarily by black male the*logians, and the other is the survival-quality-of-life tradition, developed by womanist the*logians.[14] The biblical Hagar traditions of survival have been appropriated in African American literature, biblical interpretation, and the*logical construction. The following themes of what Williams calls the biblical Hagar "quality of life traditions" have shaped African American literature and the*logy: the theme of sexual exploitation, the theme of destitution and single parentage, the theme of survival-struggle, the theme of wo/men's agency in the development of nation building, the theme of oppressed women's encounters with G*d.

> Incorporated in her naming of God is Hagar's
> confession of faith: Thou art a God of seeing

13. Horowitz et al., "Nine Killed in Shooting at Black Church in Charleston."

14. Williams, "Hagar in African American Biblical Appropriation," 171–84.

(Gen 16:13) Then in amazement she asks, "Have I really seen God and remained alive . . ." (Gen 16:13) . . . It is no wonder that black women can declare from generation from generation, "God helped us make a way out of no way. And they can easily resonate with Hagar's faith statement—"Thou art a God of Seeing."[15]

Islamophobia

While Jews and white Christians traditionally see themselves as descendants of Sarah and Isaac, Muslims and Baha'i also trace their lineage to Hagar and Ishmael. The Islamic tradition sees both Isaac and Ishmael as legitimate heirs, because when a man sleeps with a slave, the slave will be free and her son is not born a slave. Muslims also believe that it was Ishmael, not Isaac, whom Abraham was told to sacrifice. According to the Hadith, Abraham accompanied Hagar and Ishmael from Canaan to a place called Paran in the area of the Arabian Peninsula where the city of Mecca was built later. Hence, many of the rituals of the great pilgrimage, or hajj, are symbolically connected to this area in the story of Hagar and Ishmael.[16]

When they reached Paran, Abraham gave a bag of dates and a skin of water to Hagar and left her with the child in the wilderness. Hagar, frightened to be abandoned with the baby in such an isolated place, ran begging after Abraham, but he refused to stop. In terror she asks Abraham, whether G*d ordered this. When Abraham said yes, she responded: "Then G*d will not neglect us" (Gen 21:14). Hagar stayed with her son, where Abraham had left them, until the dates were eaten and the water was drunk and they grew weak

15. Williams, "Hagar in African American Biblical Appropriation," a.a.o., 182.

16. Worthington, "Hagar and Ishmael in the Wilderness."

from thirst. In the hope of finding a person, Hagar climbs every mountain to see whether a caravan is coming to rescue them, when an angel appears, digs the earth until water flows and stills their thirst. The angel promises Hagar again that G*d will make Ishmael a great nation (Gen 21:18).

Hagar and Ishmael settled in the wilderness of Paran. Therefore, Paran is seen by Islam and Baha'í as a prophecy referring to Arabia and the prophet Muhammed, because Paran was a town on the Northwestern border of Arabia where the covenant was made. In short, "The figure of Hagar that emerges from the traditions narrated in Sahib Al-Bukhari is that of a woman of exceptional faith, love, fortitude, resolution and strength of character."[17]

To sum up this exploration of the biblical Hagar/Sarah story and its footprints in American culture and politics, the biblical contrast between two wo/men representing freedom and slavery has in American politics racialized and is deeply engraved in American self-understandings. It is no longer just a literary-the*logical allegory but has become culturally engraved into American political identity as well as been naturalized in political terms.

Sex-Trafficking

What is generally overlooked in the debate on Hagar, the slave, vs. Sarah, the slave-holder, are the abusive powers and habits of Abraham who is using Sarah for his own financial profit.[18] Sex trafficking is generally defined as trading of humans for the purpose of sexual exploitation. A victim is

17. Hassan, "Islamic Hagar and Her Family," 154.

18. In addition to David Lamb cited above, see Graham, "Why Evangelicals are Arguing Online about David and Bathsheba"; González, "Abraham Broke the Law, Crossing Borders and Trafficking his Wife."

forced, in a variety of ways, into a situation of dependency on their trafficker and then used to give sexual services to others for the sake of remuneration. The story of Abraham and Sarah still needs to be recognized as such a classic sex-trafficking story.

As noted in the summary at the beginning of this chapter, when they arrive in Egypt Abram tells Sarai that she should say she is his sister and not his wife, which was half-true because they were half-siblings. This was allegedly a precautionary move, so that Abram would not be killed by the pharaoh who would want to take her into his ha-rem because of her beauty and marry her. In other words, Abram claims that because of Sarai's beauty his life is at risk. His resolution is to "give her" which means, most likely sexually, to another powerful man, the pharaoh, so that he himself will both live and prosper financially.[19]

At their arrival the Egyptians were mesmerized by Sarai's great beauty and their ruler took her into his house, remunerating Abram richly with animals and slaves. G*d's punishment is however not dealt out to Abraham for sex-trafficking his wife, but to the pharaoh who is afflicted with plagues. The *Jewish Study Bible* does not recognize this act of Abram as sex-trafficking but complains it away:

> Although Abraham is sometimes chastised for passing his beautiful wife off as his sister, it is hard to see how Sarai (whose name becomes 'Sarah' in ch. 17) would have fared better if he died at the hands of the lecherous and adulter-ous Egyptians.[20]

---

19. Schneider, *Sarah, Mother of Nations*, 30–35. See also Dijk-Hemmes, "Sarai's Exile," 227.

20. Berlin and Brettler, *Jewish Study Bible*, 31.

However, this interpretation overlooks the protest of the pharaoh who, when afflicted with plague, accuses Abram:

> What is this you have done to me! Why did you not tell me that she was your wife? Why did you say, "She is my sister," so that I took her as my wife? (Gen 12:18–19)

These words clearly indict Abram who amassed great wealth through trafficking Sarai, since there is no indication that the Egyptian ruler wanted to kill Abram in order to possess Sarai. Unfortunately, Sarai's experience is not told, because such patriarchal use of wo/men has been common sense not only at the time, but also is still so today.

Moreover, this was not the last time that Abraham does not hesitate to traffic Sarah. The second time the story is told in Gen 20:1–17 and it parallels that in Gen 12:10–20. But this time the Divinity gets directly involved. In a dream, G*d appears to King Abimelech and threatens him with death if he does not restore his wife to Abraham. The narrator assures the reader that the King has not touched Sarah because G*d prevented him from so doing. Abimelech returns Sarah and rebukes Abraham and rewards him richly with sheep and oxen and slaves (Gen 20:14). Again, Abraham is not only richly rewarded but also dignified by the Deity as a prophet.

METHODOLOGICAL—HERMENEUTICAL REFLECTIONS

Placing slave wo/men like Hagar and sexually abused wo/men like Sarah and their struggles at the center of attention, will require several shifts in our reading and interpretation of the biblical texts not only as a cultural document but also

as holy Scripture in general. First of all, it requires an understanding of the text as rhetorical construction and persuasive communication and story-telling. Understanding
texts as "storied arguments" entails that one must ask not
only what meaning such texts had and whom they sought to
persuade in their historical context but also whose interests
the cultural imprint of these texts articulates, and to what
ends they argue in the situation of their reception today.
The answer is different if one reads the Genesis texts and
the Pauline letters, or the Bible on the whole, as rhetorical
argument and cultural inscription rather than as authoritative "teachings" in its past and present contexts.

Approaching the Bible in general and the Genesis texts
as well as the Pauline letter to the Galatians in particular in
and through a focus on slave and sexually abused wo/men,
raises four key issues:

1. How should we read grammatically kyriocentric,
i.e., elite male (*kyrios* = slave-master) centered texts? In the
kyriocentric text, slave wo/men and sexually abused wo/
men are doubly invisible. On one hand, the masculine form
of the Greek word *doulos* is usually not translated as *male
slave* but rather as the generic *slave*, while the feminine
form is always translated as *female slave*. Moreover, slave
wo/men as historical agents are generally not mentioned in
the Bible. On the other hand, the gendered generic biblical
term for "woman" also does not signal that it refers only to
freeborn wo/men. Hence, studies on "women" in the bible
refer to freeborn wo/men, but they overlook that freeborn
wo/men like Sarah were sexual assets who could be traded.
To keep slave and abused freeborn wo/men in the center of
our attention requires a recognition not only of class/status
and race but also of sexuality and gender. For instance, texts
such as 1 Cor 6 and 7 raise quite different issues if one keeps
in mind that slave wo/men were the sexual property of their

male and female masters, that they often could not marry or keep their children, and that they were frequently forced into prostitution.[21] It raises the foundational question as to whether freedom was the pre-condition, the *sine qua non*, for being a morally accountable member of the *ekklēsia*. However, not only slave wo/men but also freeborn women like Sarah were the possession of their husbands and could be bartered away as sex-objects.

2. Placing slave wo/men and sexually abused slave and freeborn wo/men in the center of attention also requires that we move from a descriptive analysis of the text to a rhetorical analysis—one that pays attention not only to the author and his statements, but also to the audience to whom the text is addressed, the rhetorical problem it seeks to overcome, and the socio-political situation and symbolic universe shared by author and audience in the past and text and reader today. Generally, the label rhetoric/rhetorical is understood to refer to speech as stylistic ornament, technical means, or linguistic manipulation, that is as discourse utilizing irrational, emotional devices that are contrary to critical thinking and reasoning. However, this negative, outdated popular understanding of rhetoric must be replaced with an understanding of rhetoric as a communicative practice involving contexts, interests, values, and visions. The revival of rhetoric as critical, cultural, and intellectual discourse has both rediscovered the significance of rhetoric in the production of knowledge, in general and underscored the "rhetoricity" or "rhetoricality" of texts and interpretations, in particular. What the Genesis texts of Hagar and Sarah communicate is the cultural imprint that wo/men, whether slave or free, are in the power of Abraham, the kyrios, the lord, master, father, husband.

21. See Glancy, *Slavery in Early Christianity*.

47

3. A rhetorical approach calls for an ethics of inter-pretation and a hermeneutics of critical evaluation to be applied to biblical texts that function not only as cultural imprinted texts but also as authoritative Scripture texts in communities today. Two examples may suffice:

The Hagar-Sarah allegory in Gal 4:21–31 contrasts the slave woman and the free woman in order to illustrate enslavement to the law and freedom in Christ.[22] Although the apostle Paul is not addressing the social institution of slavery here, he reinscribes the dichotomies between slave and free as the dichotomy between "rabbinic" Judaism and "messianic" (Christian) Judaism and, whether intended or not, in the context of the dominant American culture this text works in the interest of white Christian supremacy. In so doing, the text also works theologically to divest non-messianic Judaism of its claim to religious identity as de-scended from Abraham. "Christian" freedom-identity and superiority is purchased in and through "the casting out" of the son of the slave woman. A bloody history of Christian anti-Judaism has been the consequence of this cultural bib-lical imprint. As Sheila Briggs notes, "One may argue that Paul's use of the language of slavery in figurative speech did not constitute an endorsement of slavery in the social realm; however, one cannot simply sever the rhetorical strategy from the content of the discourse."[23] Without ques-tion, the rhetoric of this Pauline text depends on metaphors taken from the institution of slavery and the sexual use of wo/men in slavery.

4. A critical feminist political interpretation also reads and interprets the Bible not only as revealed Scripture or as a literary or a historical text, but also must study the

22. Briggs, "Paul on Bondage and Freedom in Imperial Roman Society," 110–23; Briggs, "Slavery and Gender," 171–92.

23. Briggs, "Galatians," 224.

cultural-political footprints of biblical texts. The *first* task of a critical ethics and the*logy of evaluation is not simply to validate the original meaning of the text but also to assess its cultural inscriptions of meaning today and their function in our own contemporary contexts. It seeks to engender a different constellation of biblical interpretation and the cultural visions and social worlds evoked by biblical texts in order to connect them with contemporary struggles against the cultural and political imprints of slavery and sexual abuse of women. Such attention to the cultural-political reinscriptions of social and sexual slavery in and through holy Scriptures is necessary in our struggle against racist dehumanization and sexual violence against wo/men.

3

WO/MEN, POWER, AND POLITICS

The Jezebel Syndrome

ONE OF THE MOST "powerful" as well as most maligned wo/men of the Bible is the Phoenician princess and queen of Israel, Jezebel. She was married to King Ahab of Israel (1 Kgs 16:31), and Wilda Gafney argues that her correct name may have been *Izevul* which means "Ba'al Exalts," but in the process of transmission it was transformed into Jezebel meaning "Lacking Nobility" or "Fecal Matter."[1] Jezebel is not only a figure known in Jewish and Christian Scriptures but also has a vast cultural imprint. This chapter seeks to explore Jezebel's cultural-religious footprint both to get to know her better but, most importantly, to debunk the

1. Gafney, *Womanist Midrash*, 240.

biblical stereotype of her as a bad woman—a story which has been sexualized in the telling.

Most people may not have read or heard of Jezebel's story as told in 1 and 2 Kings, but her cultural footprint is enormous although it remains often subconscious. Just google Jezebel and you will find many musical entries and even a well-known feminist website in her name.[2] Janet Howe Gaines's book, *Music in the Old Bones: Jezebel Through the Ages,* has documented, moreover, the vast literary imprints of the biblical Jezebel story.[3] They can be brought to life again and again in ever new readings and re-imaginings of her story. In her book, *The Jezebel Letters; Religion and Politics in 9th Century Israel,* Eleanor Ferris Beach engages in a provocative and fascinating fictional reconstruction of the lost archive of Queen Jezebel and tells another story using a hermeneutics of reconstruction. She engages a hermeneutics of historical imagination and reconstruction using ancient documents and archeological results for composing fictitious letters of the queen to portray the queen in a different feminist historical light.[4]

HULU's adaptation of Margaret Atwood's *The Handmaid's Tale* offers a recent example of the prevalence of Jezebel's cultural imprint in American consciousness. "Jezebel's" is a place of illicit behaviors and relationships. It is a space where the most powerful men can control and abuse women for their own means and pleasures outside of the strictures that control all of the relationships in Gilead. In the eyes of powerful men, the women of "Jezebel's" have no other place or role within the society of Gilead. Hence as

2. https://jezebel.com.

3. Gaines, *Music in the Old Bones.*

4. Beach, *Jezebel Letters.*

the Commander asserts, they must "prefer it here,"[5] where the women have lost their freedom.

In HULU's version, the women of Jezebel's place are professors and intellectuals—women of intellectual power who were unable to "fit" in Gilead. Hence some have argued that HULU's version of Jezebel's is too glitzy and that in Atwood's text she portrays a sense of tawdriness that makes the place seem cheap.[6] Most disturbingly, this Jezebel stereotype is used in American culture and church to brand especially black wo/men with such a sexualized "Jezebel" label. Politically, it is therefore especially important to recognize how this biblical-cultural stereotype can be and has been used against wo/men who seek political power. I will try to disentangle this biblical-cultural stereotype of Jezebel in four steps:

First, we will look at the *historical Jezebel* and ask what we still can know about her.

In a **second** step we will explore Jezebel's religious, the*logical image and its impact in the New*Testament.

A **third** step will look at the cultural history and racist imprint of the Jezebelian stereotype that still affects black wo/men in the USA and around the world. We will also explore the religious home of this stereotype in the Black Church.

Finally, in a concluding step we will explore how the religious-cultural stereotype of "Jezebel, the foreign queen" still, consciously or not, lives on in our political discourses and especially affects wo/men of color striving for political power today. In view of the present anti-woman racist politics, it is especially important to recognize how the cultural stereotype of Jezebel, which is inspired by the Bible, is used against wo/men who seek to exercise political power today.

5. Dennis, *Handmaid's Tale.* Season 1, episode 8, "Jezebels."
6. I want to thank Mary Perez for this reference.

THE BIBLICAL-HISTORICAL SOURCE OF THE "JEZEBEL" STEREOTYPE IN I AND II KINGS

The story of Jezebel was transmitted by a group of writers and editors who are collectively identified by scholars as the Deuteronomist. One of the main purposes and goals of writing the Deuteronomistic history was to defend the worship of Jahweh and to prevent the people from worshiping other Gods, first among them Ba'al and Asherah/Astarte. The Deuteronomist's historiography is greatly biased against her because she worshiped, and was perhaps a priestess of, foreign gods.The historical and geographical setting of Jezebel's story is told in the biblical books known as 1 and 2 Kings, and the setting of her story is the midninth century BCE.[7] After David's and Solomon's reigns (ca. 1000–930 BCE), political tensions between the less prosperous South and the more well-to-do northern area of Palestine engendered a division of the country into Israel in the North and Judah in the South (ca. 930 BCE). In the Northern Kingdom, the dynasty of the Omrides emerged as the first strong dynasty. In this time period (ca. 880–840 BCE), larger walled towns and cities emerged, with a better organized political organization and the existence of lively trading relations. Literary remains from Israel's neighbors indicate that Israel was well known at the time and that the country had some influence in the region.[8]

In the biblical accounts, Jezebel is depicted as strong but wicked. She is portrayed as a powerful wo/man who defends her Gods and practices her religion as a stranger in a strange land. She does so despite the injunctions and dire warnings of the Israelite prophet and holy man, Elijah,

7. For reconstructions of Israelite history see, for instance, Miller and Hayes, *History of Ancient Israel and Judah.*

8. See Hanson, *Political History of the Bible in America,* 170–230.

who preaches an all-powerful exclusive G*d (1 Kgs 18–19). When we encounter Jezebel's name today, we usually don't think of a queen and mighty ruler but of a sexually loose or compromised woman. The story of Jezebel is alluded to or told in a number of chapters in 1 Kgs 16:31—2 Kgs 9:37. Jezebel is first mentioned in 1 Kgs 16, when the reign of king Ahab, her husband, is introduced. Ahab followed his father, king Omri, on the throne in the early ninth century BCE. He was married to Jezebel, the daughter of the king of Tyre to the North, and they had a daughter[9] and two sons, who followed him on the throne: Ahaziah, who was king for two years, and Jehoram, who reigned for twelve years. Jezebel's marriage to Ahab was a political alliance, as such marriage arrangements with neighboring dynasties like that of Ahab and Jezebel strengthened Israel's standing, influence, and power in the region. The union provided both peoples with military protection from powerful enemies, as well as valuable trade routes. Although the marriage was sound foreign policy, it was intolerable to the writers of 1 and 2 Kings. Because of Jezebel's different worship practices and religion,[10] she remains the powerful alien ruler who is not only a woman but also a worshiper of other gods.

As the daughter of the priest-king Ethbaal who ruled the coastal Phoenician (modern-day Lebanon) cities of Tyre and Sidon, Jezebel herself may have been a priestess of Ba'al and Asherah (also known as Astarte) in her homeland though we have no direct evidence of this. Nevertheless, it is safe to assume that she felt entitled with the support of her husband to continue her priestly role in her new homeland. Since she brought with her a large number of prophets

9. It is debated whether Athaliah, queen in Jerusalem and probably the most powerful woman in Israel who ruled Judah for seven years (2 Kgs 11:3), is the daughter of Ahab and Jezebel.

10. Gaines, "How Bad Was Jezebel?," 12–23, 14.

and cultic staff, she was also responsible for them in her new homeland. Because of her loyalty to her gods and cultic personal, Jezebel is seen as dangerous in the records of the Hebrew Bible/Old Testament. The queen is reviled by the Deuteronomist author not only because of her personal shortcomings and political machinations but also because she was a stranger practicing a different religion. Her active support and promotion of the priests and worshipers of Ba'al and Asherah/Astarte fueled the hostility towards her.

Rather than telling stories that portray her as a respected Israelite matron, such as the description of a wife in Proverbs,[11] the Deuteronomist relates the Naboth story through a bias that turns Jezebel's action into a crime. In a careful narrative analysis of the story about Naboth's vineyard, Patricia Dutcher-Walls shows how the narrative portrays King Ahab as a weakling who desires Naboth's vineyard but could not obtain it. Queen Jezebel in turn uses the law and her political connections with the city leaders to have Naboth indicted for blasphemy and executed in order to fulfill Ahab's wish (1 Kgs 21:11–13).

What would normally be praised as the good deed of a wife in support of her husband is now told as a crime story for which both are punished even though the city leaders, and not Jezebel, condemn Naboth to death.[12] Rather than portraying Jezebel as a caring spouse attempting to please her husband, she is portrayed as a zealous corrupt schemer who commits murder in order to fulfill the childish wishes of a weak husband, although in the Deuteronomist account

---

11. "A capable wife who can find?/She is far more precious than Jewels,/The heart of her husband trusts in her,/And he will have no lack of gain./She does him good, and not harm, all days of her life" (Prov 31:10–12).

12. Dutcher-Walls, *Jezebel*, 42–58.

it is Ahab who has provoked G*d "to anger and caused Israel to sin."[13]

JEZEBEL THE FOREIGN RELIGIOUS LEADER AND THE PROPHET ELIJAH

When Jezebel married king Ahab, she did not give up her own religion. Not only does she bring her gods and goddesses to her new country, she also brings with her the priests and cultic personnel of her homeland, whom she shelters and supports. Concerned with prospect of Israel worshiping other G*ds, the Deuteronomist writers reject Israel's foreign queen as repulsive and view her influence as dangerous. The Deuteronomist writers articulate tension between the prophet, Elijah, and the rulers, Ahab and Jezebel, in order to illustrate Jezebel's dangerous influence.

The competition and struggle between the prophet Elijah and the king and queen center on their different religious visions. Jezebel and her prophets are devotees of Ba'al and Asherah, whereas Elijah and his followers worship Jahweh or Elohim, the G*d of Israel; king Ahab seems to worship both. Whereas the name Ba'al was associated with the storm and fertility G*d Hadad and his local manifestations, Asherah/Astarte was considered the moon-goddess and often presented as a consort of Ba'al, the sun-god (Judg 3:7, 6:28, 10:6; 1 Sam 7:4, 12:10). The conflict between the prophet Elijah and the prophets of Ba'al and Asherah is told in 1 Kgs 18. Elijah asked the king to call all Israel (i.e., all men, since Jezebel is not mentioned) to gather along with the 450 prophets of Ba'al and the 400 prophets of the goddess Asherah at Mount Carmel for a contest of the G*ds. After they gathered Elijah challenged them; "if the Lord is God follow him; but if Ba'al is God, follow him" (1Kgs 18;

13. Dutcher-Walls, *Jezebel*, 44.

21) "The God who will answer with fire from the sky will be the true God!" (18:22–25)

First came the prophets of Ba'al, but despite all their prayers and offerings nothing happened. Then Elijah and the people began their ritual, and after fire fell from heaven and its flames consumed the offering, the people of Israel worshiped and declared the Lord as God (1 Kgs 18:39). Elijah then commanded: "Seize the prophets of Ba'al, let not one of them escape!" Then Elijah brought them down to the Wadi Kishon and killed them there (1Kgs 18:40). This conflict of the G*ds is at the heart of Jezebel's and Ahab's condemnation by the prophet Elijah. The animosity of the Deuteronomist writer(s) of the books of Kings against Jezebel also comes to the fore in the depiction of her cruel death. Yet, even the cruel scene of her death still reveals her dignity and majesty. Acting like a true queen in the face of death, she prepares herself carefully to meet her murderer, a traitor and the killer of her son-king (2 Kgs 9:30–37).

JEZEBEL, THE PROPHET IN THE BOOK OF REVELATION

Jezebel is mentioned a second time in the Bible in the second chapter of the book of Revelation (also called Apocalypse of John).[14] It is this book that uses the name of the queen as the name of a sexually loose woman or prostitute. John, the seer, writes to the ekklesia, or assembly, in Thyatira in Asia Minor:

> I know your works—your love, faith, service and patient endurance . . . But I have this against you: you tolerate woman Jezebel, who calls herself a

14. For further analysis, see Schüssler Fiorenza, *Book of Revelation*; Schüssler Fiorenza, "Words of Prophecy," 1–20. See especially, Pippin, "Jezebel Revamped," 32–41.

> prophet and is teaching and beguiling my ser-
> vants to practice fornication and to eat food
> sacrificed to idols. I gave her time to repent,
> but she refuses to repent of her fornication . . .
> and those who commit adultery with her I am
> throwing into great distress, unless they repent
> of her doings; and I will strike her children dead.
> (Rev 2:19–33)

John, the seer of Revelation, polemicizes rival prophets in the messages addressed to the churches in Ephesus, Pergamon, and Thyatira. Ephesus earns praise because it has rejected the false prophets and has shown hatred for their works, whereas Pergamum receives criticism for tolerating those who subscribe to the teaching of Balaam. The community of Thyatira provokes censure because it has accepted the teachings of a woman prophet whom the seer calls Jezebel. All three allowed their followers to eat food that had been sacrificed to idols as well as to participate in pagan religious festivities.

A hermeneutics of historical imagination might ask: how would these prophets have argued for the assimilation to pagan society and ritual? They might have maintained that participation in civic rituals and religion must be understood in political terms as part of one's civic duty. Didn't Paul, the great apostle, preach that faithful people should not resist civil authorities but rather give honor to whom honor is due (Rom 13)? However, John does not argue against this woman prophet because she claimed prophetic office and leadership *as a woman*. Rather, he criticizes her because he did not agree with her teachings. This indicates that it was common sense that women were accepted as prophetic leaders in the communities in Asia Minor (present day Turkey). Such influential positions and leadership of wo/men in the Asian churches is quite in keeping with the general religious and political as well as socio-cultural influence that wo/men had in Asia Minor.[15]

It is also significant that John likens this rival woman prophet in Thyatira to the Phoenician princess, Jezebel. The choice of the label "Jezebel" in Revelation might not be due so much to the fact that queen Jezebel supported pagan religious practices and opposed the prophets of Yahweh. It may more likely allude to the high status and wealth of the woman prophet, referring to Jezebel's backing of some 850 prophets of Baal and Asherah/Astarte. Like Jezebel who as queen had great power in Israel (cf. 1 Kgs 16–21 and 2 Kgs 9–10), the prophet named Jezebel is critiqued because of her power and wealth. "Her fornication is less likely a literal charge, than John's metaphor to describe her positive relations with Greco-Roman society."[16]

In sum, in the Hebrew Bible and the Christian New Testament, Jezebel is portrayed as queen and powerful prophet, whose followers are committing "adultery" with her—a biblical metaphor for unfaithfulness and worship of other gods. Hence, it is more than surprising that during the time of slavery in America, the image of Jezebel, the whore, became the controlling elite white male imagination of Black womanhood.[17]

THE CULTURAL RACIAL-SEXIST JEZEBEL STEREOTYPE AND IMPRINT

As Christine Eck notes, since the times of slavery, three stereotypes have defined and dehumanized Black wo/men: The Aunt Jemima Mammy, the Jezebel, and the Sapphire

15. See my book *Book of Revelation*.

16. Frankfurter, "Revelation to John," 471.

17. Hill Collins, "Controlling Images and Black Women's Oppression" 266–73.

stereotypes. Whereas the Mammy stereotype portrays black wo/men as cheerful, good, and faithful household "slaves," the Sapphire label caricaturizes black wo/men as domineering, angry, and masculine, and the Jezebel label indicts them as sexually loose wo/men.[18] Jezebel's cultural imprint keeps alive the stereotype of the black wo/man in slavery as hypersexual. The European colonizers of the sixteenth century and beyond perceived scantily clad natives, tribal dances, and polygamy as lewd, hyper-sexed, and subhuman. Black women were labeled as "Jezebels" and men as brutish, uncivilized rapists. Hence, it was justified to colonize and enslave them.

Psychological studies have shown that the Jezebel stereotype portrays black wo/men as seductive, promiscuous, and sexually voracious. For instance, Morgan Chambers Jerald has shown in her dissertation, which explored the influence of the Jezebel stereotype on Black wo/men's sexual health, that Black wo/men who endorse this stereotype suffer detrimental, negative consequences in their sexual relationships.[19] Sociology professor David Pilgrim of Ferris State University discusses how Black women have been socially branded with this enduring Jezebel stereotype.[20] Black wo/men have been portrayed as alluring, tempting, and lewd, whereas white wo/men are portrayed as ladies who are examples of purity, models of self-control and modesty.

Unfortunately, Emancipation and Reconstruction did not stop the victimization and sexual stereotyping of Black wo/men. The portrayal of Black wo/men as hypersexualized Jezebels continued through the Jim Crow period and is still at work today. According to David Pilgrim, the portrayal of

18. Eck, "Three Books, Three Stereotypes," 11–24.
19. Chambers Jerald, "Respectable Women."
20. Pilgrim, "Jezebel Stereotype."

Black wo/men as Jezebels has continued in American mate-rial culture, documented by the Jezebel images collected in the Jim Crow Museum of Racist Memorabilia. For instance, a metal nutcracker depicts a topless Black woman, and the nut to be crushed is to be placed in her crotch under her skirt.[21] The Jezebel stamp of Black wo/men permeates also popular music. According to Taylor Gordon, "If an African American woman isn't being portrayed as a finger snapping, wise cracking southern cook who doubles as a maid, she's usually a Jezebel . . . Most hip hop and rap music videos are filled with Jezebels who are competing for the rap star's attention or already busy stripping down to their birthday suits to make him happy."[22]

In *Jezebel Unhinged: Loosing the Black Female Body in Religion and Culture,* Tamura Lomax focuses on the de-ployment of the Jezebel stereotype both in popular culture as well as in the Black church and popular Black religion. As Lomax notes, the book examines:

> how the discourse on black womanhood pro-duced by white capitalist racism, sexism, het-erosexism, and classism birthed a simultaneous jezebelian ho' discourse in black communities and institutions—to the point, where "hoism" . . . seems normative, even within the Black Church which constructs and peddles its own brand of ho theology and draws on and helps solidify the jezebelian metanarrative.[23]

In short, Tamura Lomax's book challenges the prac-tice of distinguishing between acceptable and unacceptable wo/men or between "hos" and "ladies." She argues that contemporary Black church culture cultivates the Jezebel

21. Pilgrim, "Jezebel Stereotype."
22. Gordon, "Black Women in the Media."
23. Lomax, *Jezebel Unhinged*, xii.

stereotype to proclaim divine approval of the lady and the rejection of the "ho" in order to preserve gender hierarchy and heteronormativity in Black communities and institutions. Hence, the Jezebel stereotype must be dismantled and its the*logical construction of the "lady" that needs to be questioned.

THE "JEZEBEL SPIRIT" AND THE VILIFICATION OF WO/MEN SEEKING POWER

The political cultural imprint of Jezebel's negative image in the Bible continues to leave its mark in contemporary American political discourses, which are still heavily biblically typed. The polemics against and mistrust of Muslims, for instance, is today fueled by the fear of other religions, whereas the polemics against Mexicans and immigrants reflects the historical Protestant-Catholic split. The president's anti-Mexican-immigrant tirades have had a deadly consequence in the El Paso shootings.[24] Previously Trump also attacked four female minority Congressmembers, US Representatives Ayanna Pressley, Ilhan Omar, Rashida Tlaib, and Alexandria Ocasio-Cortez, telling them that they should go back to "the totally broken and crime infested places from which they came," although all four of them were raised in the US.[25]

What do these political vignettes have to do with Jezebel? Asking this question, one immediately thinks of Jezebel, the stranger and immigrant queen. Her history in America has served as a negative image of and label for Black wo/men in slavery and its imprint lasts today. Moreover, Jezebel seems to have an extensive presence on

24. Attanasio et al., "Police."

25. Mason and Cornwell, "Trump Defiant as Lawmakers Blast his 'Racist' Attacks on Four Congresswomen."

the web. Many websites under her name associate Jezebel's name with spiritual political warfare and demonology. This discourse on spiritual warfare is a neo-charismatic spiritual discourse that envisions Jezebel having a key role in the success or failure of the spiritual welfare of the nation. A core concept in this third wave spiritual discourse is "spiritual mapping." Spiritual mapping charts spaces such as neighborhoods, cities, and whole countries as either living in the divine light or demonic darkness. O'Donnell argues:

> . . . despite (or because of) its conception of spiritual warfare, spiritual mapping privileges America and its national integrity—the integrity of the 'body' of (normative Christian) America—as the lynchpin of its cosmic war.[26]

In spiritual warfare, spaces of darkness speak of the absence of G*d and signify the presence of Satan. Moral darkness in believers is produced by sin. Darkness even covers organizations and territories, one of which is occupied by Jezebel. Domains of darkness are signifying the absence of G*d. Hence, Jezebel, the queen of darkness destabilizes the evangelical-fundamentalist version of America as G*d's and Christ's very own territory.

Jezebel's displacement of "Christian America" is articulated through readings of the biblical narratives about her idolatry, which as O'Donnell illustrates,

> Is herein connected to her upbringing in another (illegitimate) culture and her unwillingness to submit to the (legitimate) culture of her husband, reinforcing links between disruption of patriarchal norms and failures of cultural assimilation.[27]

26. O'Donnell, "Body Politic(s) of the Jezebel Spirit," 240–55, 241.
27. O'Donnell, "Body Politic(s)," 247.

Rebellion against monotheistic hegemony is Jezebel's central crime and threat to Christian America. She threatens G*d's authority as male, monotheistic, legitimate, and native authority. With her own female, foreign, polytheistic, illegitimate authority the biblical figure of Jezebel actively disrupts the systems of hetero-kyriarchal monotheism. Her "otherness" is threefold: as idolater she challenges monotheistic truth, as foreigner she threatens Christian hegemonic American identity, and claiming her power envisioned in American culture as a black slave woman, she displaces white male kyriarchal supremacy. This contorted image of Jezebel can easily be used against wo/men claiming their power to political office.

4

THE THREE BIBLICAL MIRYAMS (MARYS) SAY #METOO

MIRYAM, THE SISTER OF Moses, Miryam, the Mother of Jesus, and Miryam from Magdala, also called Mary Magdalene, are probably the biblical women best known to Christian and/or Jewish readers. When asked to name wo/men in the Bible, students will mention at least one of the three. To associate these biblical wo/men with the "#MeToo" movement, however, goes against the grain of biblical piety. The #MeToo movement (or MeToo movement), is a movement against sexual harassment, and sexual physical and mental abuse. Activist and survivor Tarana Burke founded the Me Too movement as part of her non-profit Just Be, Inc. to advocate for survivors of sexual assault with a particular focus on young black women. The hashtag #MeToo was then popularized on social media in 2017 by actress Alyssa Milano. While the #MeToo movement[1] is known for its struggle against sexual abuse, I want to broaden it here to include also mental and religious-spiritual abuse of power.

Jewish feminists have rediscovered Miryam as one of the leaders in the exodus from slavery in Egypt. Miryam, the mother of Jesus is not only venerated by Christians but also by Muslims. She has most recently received public recognition at Christmas time as one of the "caged refugees" of public nativity scenes.[2] Miryam of Magdala in turn is popularly known through the 1970 rock opera *Jesus Christ Superstar,* singing "I loved him so!" and through Dan Brown's controversial book *The Da Vinci Code.*[3] However, in the Gospels she is not characterized by her relationship to a male figure but carries the name of her town of origin, Magdala, an ancient city on the shore of the Sea of Galilee in Israel.

All three biblical "Miryam/Mariam/Mary" figures are also paradigms of wo/men's public leadership in society and religion. While no sexual abuse is told about Miryam, she experienced Divine physical abuse being punished with leprosy. While Mary of Nazareth, the teenage Mother of Jesus is venerated by Roman Catholics as "immaculate" and/or "pure and without sin," Mary Magdalene has been seen as a sinner, lover or wife of Jesus, and a whore.

1. Nicolaou and Smith, "#MeToo Timeline To Show How Far We've Come—& How Far We Need To Go."

2. Salo, "Church under Fire for Nativity Scene Depicting Jesus, Mary and Joseph as Caged Refugees"; See also: Blackmore. "Pope's New Nativity Scene Raises Awareness of Worldwide Refugee Crisis."

3. Brown, *Da Vinci Code.*

MIRYAM—LEADER OF HER PEOPLE

Miryam is a biblical celebrated leader in Jewish feminist traditions. Ellen Frankel's commentary on the Torah renames the Five Books of Moses as the "Five Books of Miriam."[4] Miryam seems to be the younger sister of Aaron and the older sister of Moses (Num 26:59). It is generally assumed that the unnamed sister of Moses mentioned in Exod 2:4 is Miryam, since the Greek (Septuagint) Text of Exod 6:20 mentions three children of Ambram and Jochebed who "bore to him Aaron and Moses, and Miriam, their sister" (cf. also Num 26:59; 1 Chr 5:29 and Micah 6:4). In the Song of the Sea (Exod 15:20) Miryam is called a prophet who is the leader of her people in celebrating G*d's saving activity in their exodus from the bondage of Egypt:

> And the prophet Miryam, Aaron's Sister took a hand-drum in her hand and all the women went out after her with hand-drums and with dances. And Myriam sang to the all: Sing to the Holy One, for s/he has triumphed gloriously, horse and rider s/he has thrown into the sea.[5]

Among others, Phyllis Trible has argued that the entire "Song of the Sea" not just one verse was ascribed to Miriam and the women of Israel. Later redactors (editors) who were intent on elevating Moses, took the song right of her mouth and gave it to him—to Moses, the inarticulate one—in company with the sons of Israel. Thus, they constructed an ending for the Exodus story that contradicted the older tradition.[6] According to Carol Meyers, Miryam is the first woman to receive the title "prophet" in the Bible and one of the few women who is not identified either as mother or

---

4. Frankel, *Five Books of Miriam.*
5. Translation by Gaffney, *Womanist Midrash*, 95.
6. Trible, "Bringing Myriam out of the Shadows," 19f.

wife. Rather the "canonical image of Miriam is of someone 'who challenges authority and who becomes a spokesperson for God.'"[7]

We encounter Miryam again in Num 12:2 where a central question of ultimate authority "Has G*d not spoken with us also?" is placed on her lips. The historical-literary context of Num 12:2 is still the journey of the Israelites through the desert after the exodus from Egypt. But the concrete textual occasion for Miryam's and Aaron's question is disputed by exegetes. If the central the*logical question, "has G*d spoken only with Moses?" is seen as a rhetorical question, a negative answer is expected: of course, G*d has spoken not only with Moses, but also with her. But such a negative answer is cut off by the text. G*d comes personally in a cloud to affirm that "he" speaks with Moses only, "from mouth to mouth," and "not in riddles."

Moses is the sole bearer of revelation, and whoever questions his revelatory authority must reckon with severe consequences. This then happens to Miryam. G*d's wrath falls on her alone, and not on Aaron, although both have challenged Moses. YHWH, moving away from the place of revelation, leaves Miryam stricken with a skin disease. In short, it is Miryam and not Aaron who is punished with leprosy. The text further excuses Aaron by making him the witness to Miryam's punishment. Aaron pleads with Moses to intervene on Miryam's behalf, and Moses in turn begs YHWH to heal Miryam. Thus, the male leadership figures are rhetorically approved by G*d, while Miryam the female leadership figure experiences divine rejection. In punishing Miryam, YHWH refers to the right of the patriarch of the house to punish his daughters and to exclude Miryam from the community for seven days. However, the people do not abandon their leader. The people wait until Miryam

7. Meyers, "Miriam, Music, and Miracles," 27–48, 27.

has completed her punishment and returned to the community before continuing on their way through the desert. The story of Miryam, which is closely bound up with that of the people, thus reveals to us its radical-democratic roots.

A detailed rhetorical-critical analysis of the Miryam texts, can show that texts like this text or Deut 24:8–9 represent a tradition that is favoring Moses and asserts that any rivalry with the revelatory authority of Moses is to be rejected.[8] At this point malestream scholarship tends to avoid the central the*logical problem posed by the text and to overlook the negative answer given by G*d to the question "has G*d not spoken with us also?" This tendency to relativize this difficult text rhetorically or historically in terms of other texts, or to concentrate on textual variants, source material, redaction, and the socio-historical context in religion, implicates scholarship in the rhetorical violence against wo/men.

What is so set aside and silenced is the central the*logical problem that echoes through the history of biblical religion and cultures: are wo/men—Jewish wo/men, Muslim wo/men, or Christian wo/men—second-class citizens? Is G*d a patriarchal God of kyriarchy to whom wo/men must remain masochistically subject? Does G*d punish the wo/men who claim their own authority, their own power, and their own leadership potential, and exercise

8. Rapp, *Miriam*, 393: "Thus when the prophecy of Miriam and Aaron is spoken of, the reference is to religious and political authorities in postexilic Judah that stood up as representatives of the religious, political, and economic interests of the population of the land against the 'returnees' who saw themselves as the sole Mosaic authority and of 'Persian beneficence.' These came with the claim to represent the only legitimate form of YHWH-faith and were also sent, under the leadership of Ezra and Nehemiah, to stabilize Judah politically, depress its economy (cf., *inter alia*, Nehemiah 5), and shape its religion" (my translation).

these actively? Like the biblical text, scholars and religious officials answer Miryam's question with the claim to the authority of scriptural revelation to exercise such violence.

Anyone who rebels against such violent religious authority and says "me too" is excluded from the community, not only for a time, but often forever.[9] The upstarts are given a choice: either do not ask Miryam's question at all and bow oneself unquestioningly before the authority of revelation or abandon religion as the space of violence against wo/men. However, a critical feminist perspective of liberation suggests another way, a third possibility for avoiding such spiritual violence.

The question whether wo/men are explicitly and often violently excluded by divine fiat from political and religious power and authority as public leaders, agents of revelation, or authority figures has never been silenced despite all the violent attempts to silence wo/men. In short, the questions "Did G*d speak only with Moses, Amos, Jesus, Augustine, Luther, the pope, the Senate, or the president? Did G*d not speak with us wo/men and other marginalized people also?" remain the central political and religious questions still today. A hermeneutics of suspicion and critical deconstruction of the text is therefore appropriate.[10]

Biblical scholars point out that the biblical text uses the figure of "G*d" to lend authority to the writers own authorial interests. They argue that the divine words in the text are culturally and historically conditioned and that the text seeks to intervene in power struggles that stem from a kyriarchal mentality and therefore inculcate male dominance. Feminist the*logy appeals to the methods of exegetical, historical, and hermeneutical biblical scholarship for its hermeneutics of suspicion and its critical deconstruction of

9. See my book, *Jesus: Sophia's Child, Miriam's Prophet.*
10. See my book, *Wisdom Ways.*

the text, which questions in principle every kind of fundamentalist way of reading the text. Since the dominant established interpretation cannot see the misogynistic and anti-democratic character of its view of history and of revelation, it is not able to work through the the*logical implications of Miryam's "me too" question: "Has G*d not spoken with us also?" as long as its perspectives remain elitist-male and Eurocentric-kyriarchal.

Only when Miryam's question "Has G*d not also spoken with us?" is answered positively will it be possible to publicly acknowledge as sin the violence exercised in the name of G*d against the authority and public leadership of wo/men. This would require a transformation of the "biblical-cultural imprint" of political leadership in the United States. Only if and when such a public confession is rendered, will it be possible also culturally to reject the history of violence exercised in the name of G*d, the violence that resulted in the persecution of witches, anti-Judaism, slavery, and colonial exploitation.

This brutal answer to Miryam's question placed by the biblical text in the mouth of G*d has engendered religious-spiritual abuse.[11] It has shaped not only religious but also political reality, especially in societies like the US that are historically inspired by the biblical record. Thus, Miryam's question reclaims the authority of wo/men and other marginalized people and this religious claim is also a fundamental political claim. It is not only human-kyriarchal authority that is thus called into question. It is, rather, also biblical talk about G*d's own self that is in crisis. This history of violent silencing needs to be recognized for what it is: kyriarchal religious and political power abusing the name of G*d.

---

11. ENCA, "Religious Abuse Addressed at Summit."

Feminist biblical scholarship has also pointed to at least traces of a biblical tradition that recognizes Miryam as a prophet of equal rank and is democratically oriented to the people of Israel. The tradition represents Miryam as a prophet who inhabits a central place in Israel's covenant with G*d. Miriam is seen as prophet in a twofold sense. She acts as a prophet by interpreting history in terms of G*d's liberation (Exod 15), and her prophetic leadership in turn is proclaimed by G*d's own self as the core piece of Israelite knowledge of salvation (Micah 6:4).

Numbers 20:1–13 in turn places emphasis on the people, their liberation from slavery and their experience of G*d's saving action that echoes in all the Miryam texts. Hence, the perspective of the people is central to an understanding of Num 20. Ursula Rapp summarizes the significance of this text as follows: "With the narrative of Miriam's death her political and theological(!) significance among the leadership elite is sustained."[12] This text also reveals interest in a form of democratic leadership for Israel that is strongly oriented to the desires and needs of the people.[13] Miryam thus is not only connected to the #MeToo movement but also to the ecological movement.

This alternative Miryam tradition, which emphasizes her prophetic and salvation-historical role, has been buried and can only with difficulty be drawn out of the text through a rhetorical-critical analysis of the tensions and contradictions inscribed in the text. Here Moses appears as the representative of Torah and divine legal ordinances, Aaron as representative of cult and worship, and Miriam as prophetic representative of a radical-democratic ethos. But this division of leadership offices must not be understood in terms of a framework of gender difference if the structure

12. Rapp, *Mirjam*, 386.
13. Rapp, *Mirjam*, 392.

of order, ritual, and ethos is not to be the*logically gendered again, with institutional and cultic office assigned to men and religious-ecstatic experience understood as ingrained in female nature.

Miryam represents the the*logical claim that at the heart of the saving event a radical democratic ethos can be not only the*logically contemplated, but historically realized. To put it another way, divine saving action is essentially a radical democratic action whose goal is the well-being of all without exception. Miryam is the biblical representative who gives the*logical expression to this claim.

But this alternative Miryam tradition must not be misused as an apologetic excuse for the sorrowful tradition of exclusion that is paradigmatically associated with the figure of Miryam. The critical question that Num 12 poses to our talk about G*d may not be misused in favor of a buried positive Miryam tradition in order to avoid responsibility for biblical traditions of injustice and for the Christian history of violence. Instead, it must be kept alive as a "dangerous memory" that empowers us the*logically to articulate G*d's action as saving action also for wo/men and other marginal people.

Jewish feminist the*logy has taken up the Miryam tradition in midrash, art, and liturgy and given it life again, finding a central place for Miryam in the Passover celebration. This celebration announces: G*d has also spoken with us wo/men. In such feminist celebrations Miryam is honored as the central figure in G*d's saving action. Her cup stands alongside that of Elijah and points to the revelatory authority of wo/men, which is still not realized.

The Jewish author Esther Broner has made Miryam's question the central question in her Passover Haggadah:

> Mother, asks the clever daughter:
> Who are our mothers?

73

Who are our grandmothers?
What is our history?
Give us our name. Recite our family tree.

Mother, asks the bad daughter,
If I learn my history
won't I be angry?
Won't I be bitter like Miriam
who was robbed of her prophecy?

Mother, asks the simple daughter,
If Miriam lies buried in the sand
why must we dig up her bones?
Why must we remove her from the sun and stone
where she belongs?

The one who knows not how to ask
has no past,
has no present,
has no future
without knowing her mothers,
without understanding her anger,
without knowing her questions.[14]

MIRYAM OF NAZARETH: #METOO?

At Christmastime in 2019 a United Methodist church in California drew press attention for its nativity scene picturing Jesus, Mary, and Joseph as refugees in separate cages. Three years earlier, the pope's nativity scene in St. Peter's Square sought to draw attention to the worldwide refugee crisis in a similar way.[15] It brought to worldwide attention that the baby Jesus was a child of refugees. Like so many

14. Broner and Nimrod, *Telling*, 198.

15. Blakemore, "Pope's New Nativity Scene Raises Awareness of Worldwide Refugee Crisis."

refugees today Mary and Joseph had to flee to Egypt to save the baby's life.

> Now after they [the three Magi] had left, an An-
> gel of the Lord appeared to Joseph in a dream
> and said: "Get up, take the child and his mother
> and flee to Egypt and remain there until I tell
> you; for Herod is about to search for the child,
> to destroy him." (Matt 2:13)

As liberation theologies of all colors have insisted, the historical woman Mary of Nazareth is not the Mary of the "holy pictures."[16] Nor is she the Mary of the "happily-ever after fairy-tale ending" of Christmas lore and ecclesiastical malestream projection. She is a poor woman and refugee.

Robert McAffee Brown has transmitted a Catholic liturgical exchange in an unspecified Latin American coun-try, which compares the Mary "of the holy pictures" with the poor pregnant teenage Mary of the Magnificat:

Priest:	Tell us about Mary of the holy pictures.
Response:	(displaying a picture): Here she is. She is standing on a crescent moon. She is wearing a crown. She has rings on her fingers. She has a blue robe embroi-dered with gold.
Priest:	That *does* sound like a different Mary from the Mary of the song! Do you think the picture has betrayed the Mary of the Song?

. . .

Response:	The Mary who said that God "has put down the mighty from their thrones" would not be wearing a crown.

Corporate Response: Take off her crown! . . .

16. Brown, *Theology in a New Key*, 99–100.

| Response: | The Mary who said that God "has filled the hungry with good things" would not have left the people who were still hungry to wear a silk robe embroidered with gold. |

Corporate Response: Take off her robe!

Anguished Response: But, Father, this is not right! (embarrassedly) We're, we're doing a striptease of the Virgin.

Priest:	Very well, if you don't like the way Mary looks in this picture, what do you think the Mary of the song would look like?
Response:	The Mary of the song would not be standing on the moon. She would be standing in the dirt and dust where we stand.
Response:	The Mary of the song would not be wearing a crown. She would have an old hat like the rest of us, to keep the sun from causing her to faint.
Response:	The Mary of the song would not be wearing a silk robe embroidered with gold. She would be wearing old clothes like the rest of us.

Embarrassed Response: Father, it may be awful to say this, but it sounds as though Mary would look just like me! My feet are dirty, my hat is old, my hands are rough, and my clothes are torn.

Although the anguished voice of the dialogue referring to the striptease of the Virgin alludes to sexual violence, it still exhibits a moralistic male perspective. Nonetheless, this voice articulates an "opening" for addressing issues of sexual violence which the priest eludes rather than addresses. He does so by turning the discussion back to the Mary of the Magnificat song who does not speak specifically from the perspective of a pregnant woman. The*logical imagination still sees Mary as the sexually untainted "pure" virgin and mother. Mary is not imagined as a raped, molested, and sexually violated young woman. Rather she is understood as a poor woman and contrasted with the mighty and rich. Insofar as the*logy does not address the question of sexual violence against women and Mary's possible subjection to it, the Mary of the "holy pictures" lives on in the image of Mary as an impoverished and hungry woman.

The infancy stories of the gospels and especially the Magnificat, which are generally held to provide a revelatory frame for liberation theological reflections foster such an elision of possible sexual violence suffered by Mary although they do not completely eradicate traces of it. They speak of poverty, marginality, and hunger but not of the specific danger of sexual violence against women in occupied territories.

The infancy stories of Jesus in the Gospels might have been wo/men's stories that were retold again and again before they received their written form in Matthew's and Luke's gospel.[17] Although written down they have never been brought to closure. They have been repeated, amplified, and totally changed in countless ways and still are told today at Christmastime.

As "Christmas" stories these stories have become privatized, racialized, and functionalized. The Bethlehem of the Christmas stories is a legendary place of singing angels and the babe in the manger. Like Santa's shop at the North Pole, the stable of Bethlehem with the sweet baby boy have become part of the cultural repertoire that fosters holiday spending. Together with the shepherds in the fields, his adoring mother sustains the romantic emotions of the holiday spirit. Christmas has become the foremost feast of shopping in the global village. For the most part women are the high priestesses of this consumer ritual, not only in

17. For literature and exegetical discussion of these texts see: Brown, *Birth of the Messiah* and Horsley, *Liberation of Christmas.*

the United States which consumes more than 70 percent of the world's resources but also in the whole industrialized world.

Biblical scholarship points out that already the infancy narratives of the canonical Gospels Matthew and Luke began to turn the story about the pregnant Miryam into a fairy tale—or as scholars say—into mythical or miraculous accounts that are historically suspect. Critical exegesis has sought to trace the literary development of the two quite different versions of the canonical Gospels and to contextualize them in the religious cultural ambiance of the first century. In contrast to biblical literalists who insist on the historical facticity of the infancy narratives, critical scholars stress their religious-symbolic meaning and spiritualized reality. Thus, both approaches, the literalist and the scholarly, sustain the cultural "Christmas" fairy tale mentality.

In Luke's account, Mary does not remain alone with her anxieties but seeks support from another woman, Elizabeth. Filled with the Holy Spirit, who exalts the violated and makes the fruit of illegitimacy holy, the two women rejoice in G*d's liberating action. In the Magnificat, the pregnant Mary enunciates G*d's salvation and well-being to the humiliated and downtrodden. The future of G*d's well-being for all without exception is not to be awaited passively. It is being born among us today, from our flesh and blood, from our commitments and struggles for justice. It becomes born as the hope for those who are without hope.

To place the agency of Mary, the "single" mother, into the center of our attention seeks to interrupt the kyriocentric celebration of the eternal feminine, the image of the "white Lady." Such a feminist move is dangerous in the eyes of both ecclesiastical and political authorities. The late professor Jane Schaberg has been ferociously attacked and vilified by the Catholic right because of her book on the illegitimacy of Jesus, in which she argues that the Gospels indicate some awareness that Mary was raped, possibly by a Roman centurion, and conceived Jesus.[18]

The "dangerous memory" of the young woman and teenage mother Miryam of Nazareth, who was probably not more than 12–13 years old, pregnant, frightened, and single, who sought help from another woman, places her in the company of wo/men who have said "me too" in ways that subvert the tales of mariological fantasy and cultural femininity. In the center of the Christian story stands not the lovely White Lady of artistic and popular imagination, kneeling in adoration before her son. Rather it is the young pregnant woman, living in occupied territories and struggling against victimization and for survival and dignity. It is she who joins the movement #MeToo holding out the promise of solidarity with all those abused. Seen as a survivor of rape, Mary joins the countless wo/men ravished by soldiers in war and occupation. The raped wo/men of Sudan, Bangladesh, Kuwait, Sarajevo, or Iraq intrude into the mythology of the perpetual virgin and Queen of Heaven. It is she who holds out the offer of untold possibilities for a different future of abused wo/men. As the late womanist scholar Dr. Katie G. Cannon has underscored, central for struggling communities such as the Black Church are three things: first, the notion of the victim as an *imago dei (image of G*d)*, second that the victim demands justice and love, and last but not least solidarity in community.[19]

In Luke's account, Mary does not remain alone with her anxieties but seeks support from another woman,

18. Schaberg, *Illegitimacy of Jesus;* Schaberg, "Feminist Interpretations of the Infancy Narrative of Matthew," 35–62; Reilly, "Jane Schaberg, Raymond E. Brown, and the Problem of the Illegitimacy of Jesus," 57–80.

19. Canon, *Black Womanist Ethics.*

Elizabeth. Filled with the Holy Spirit who exalts the violated and makes the fruit of so-called illegitimacy holy, the two wo/men rejoice in G*d's liberating action. In the Magnificat, the pregnant Mary promises G*d's salvation and well-being to the humiliated and downtrodden. The future of G*d's well-being for all without exception is not to be awaited passively. It is being born among us today, from our flesh and blood, from the commitments and struggles of the discipleship community of equals for the justice and well-being of the *basileia*, G*d's alternative world.

To place the agency of Miryam, the "single" teenage mother, who joins #MeToo into the center of our attention is dangerous in the eyes of both ecclesiastical and political authorities who protect predatory, sexually-abusing churchmen and men of state. The ongoing clergy abuse scandal has focused on the abuse of boys and young men but has not even began to address the abuse of girls and young wo/men. Such abuse is not only rampant in Roman Catholicism but also in other Christian, Jewish, and Muslim religious organizations.

MIRYAM OF MAGDALA

The third wo/man called Miryam is Mary Magdalene. Although her story and that of the other Jewish wo/men disciples of Jesus who heeded the call of Divine Wisdom is not very extensive, we still can find traces of their discipleship in the Gospels. The Gospel traditions still transmit some of the names of the women disciples who followed Jesus from Galilee to Jerusalem. These women are said to have been not only the primary witnesses to Jesus's execution and burial but also remembered as the first who proclaimed Jesus's resurrection. Mary of Magdala was the most prominent of these Galilean wo/men disciples. According to tradition she was called "the apostle to the apostles." The witness of Mary of Magdala and the other wo/men disciples insists that G*d and the resurrected One can only be found among the Living Ones.[20]

Mary of Magdala and the other wo/men disciples were commissioned to go and tell the "brothers," "Jesus is alive and going ahead to Galilee." The wo/men disciples are sent to the male disciples to proclaim the good news of the Living One. They are called to empower the community of the Living One. The Living One is going ahead—not going away—so the wo/men in the Gospels and we with them are told. Fear of brutal state violence could not stop the witness of Mary of Magdala and the other wo/men disciples.

Galilean women were not only decisive for the extension of the Jesus movement to gentiles but also for the very continuation of this movement after Jesus's arrest and execution. Jesus's Galilean wo/men disciples did not flee after his arrest but stayed in Jerusalem witnessing his execution and burial. These Galilean women were also the first to articulate their experience of the powerful goodness of G*d who did not leave the crucified Jesus in the grave but raised him from the dead. The early Christian confession that "Jesus the Nazarene who was executed on the cross was raised" is, according to the resurrection story of Mark 16:1–6, 8a, revealed in a vision first to the Galilean women disciples of Jesus.

In all likelihood, the Galilean disciples of Jesus fled after his arrest from Jerusalem and went back home to Galilee. Because of their visionary-ecstatic experiences, those wo/men who remained in the capital came to the conviction that G*d had vindicated Jesus and his ministry. They, therefore, felt empowered to continue the movement and work of Jesus, the Resurrected One. They probably sought

20. See my book, *In Memory of Her,* 105–59.

to gather together the dispersed disciples and friends of Jesus who lived in and around Jerusalem—wo/men disciples like Mary of Magdala, Martha of Bethany, the unnamed wo/man who had anointed Jesus, the mother of John Mark who had a house in Jerusalem, or Mary, the mother of Jesus. Some of these wo/men probably also moved back, very soon, to Galilee, their native country.

The traditions about Mary of Magdala and the wo/men disciples also bespeak the misogyny that wo/men face who dare to assume public leadership and compete for the presidency: Hillary Clinton, Kamala Harris, Elizabeth Warren to mention a few. In Christian the*logy, Mary of Magdala, the apostle to the apostles, has been turned into the repentant sinner and "most chaste" whore, the sexuate wo/man who is in love with Jesus and teaches him feminine ways of being. This stereotype of Mary Magdalene was solidified by Pope Gregory the Great (540–604). He praised Mary Magdalene as the example of repentance and conversion to the people of Rome who were suffering from famine, plague, and war. As Susan Haskins writes:

> And so, the transformation of Mary Magdalene was complete. From the Gospel figure, with her active role as the herald of the New Life—the Apostle to the Apostles—she becomes the redeemed whore and Christianity's model of repentance, a manageable and controllable figure and effective weapon and instrument of propaganda against her own sex.[21]

The stories of the wo/men disciples have not just been forgotten but Miryam of Magdala, the apostle to the apostles, has also been culturally and theologically sexualized and feminized. Today, Christian churchmen

21. Haskins, *Mary Magdalen*, 96–97.

and theologians no longer emphasize the sinfulness of the "fallen woman" Mary Magdalene, but rather degrade her leadership by continuing to insist in many churches and different parts of the world that wo/men cannot lead churches and become ordained because Jesus chose only men as apostles. Popular culture continues to reinforce the traditional Christian stereotype of Mary Magdalene and wo/men in general as either temptresses or lovers of great men. Mary Madalene is their prime example. In books such as Kasantzakis's *The Last Temptation*, in films such as Scorsese's *The Last Temptation of Christ,* or in musicals such as *Jesus Christ Superstar,* Mary Magdalene has become degraded from an apostle, leader, and witness of new life to a symbol of female sinfulness and a feminine stereotype of self-sacrificing love for a great man. Contemporary books and stories about Mary of Magdala could be summed up with the refrain of *Jesus Christ Superstar,* "I love him so." Modern music, literature, and art portray her as the lover of Jesus or as his wife whose total being exists in loving self-sacrifice and admiration.

The cult of femininity is all-pervasive in the labels given Miryam of Magdala: the picture of Mary Magdalene as the wild prostitute, the wo/man sinner who becomes the lover of Jesus and is saved, or of the wo/man full of evil spirits reinforces the cultural ideology of femininity in a time of political backlash against wo/men, a time of international sex trade and clergy abuse, a time when wo/men in the churches say "#MeToo," and sadly enough a time in which young wo/men are still told that their divine calling in life is the calling to marriage and motherhood.

In her book *The Mary Magdalene Cover Up,* Esther de Boer disagrees with Susan Haskins's conclusion that

> at a stroke, Gregory the Great resolved all early
> Christian wrestling with Mary Magdalene as

first witness to the resurrection through his picture of her as a penitent . . . with his picture of
Mary Magdalene as a penitent Gregory the Great
is said deliberately to have shown all women
their place . . . But what is more important is
that Gregory the Great's image of Mary Magdalene as a penitent and a reformed prostitute has
nothing to do with the Mary who appears in the
early sources . . . [it] is a construct [that] must be
rejected not only on moral but also on historical
grounds.[22]

Despite such disparagement and cooptation of
Miryam of Magdala in Western Christianity, the memory
of Mary of Magdala's discipleship and her mission to the
"brethren" still survives and is, again, very much alive.
Because of extensive feminist research it is gaining new
strength today.

In the past five decades, critical feminist biblical studies have shown that Miryam of Magdala was not a sinner or
"fallen woman" but a leading member of the Jewish movement that has been named after Jesus. Like Jesus and the
other wo/men disciples she moved from Galilee to Jerusalem, there witnessing Jesus's arrest, execution, and burial,
and as the main witness to the resurrection, she became the
apostle to the apostles.

Thus, Miryam of Magdala has become the symbol of
hope for many, the image that challenges those who fear
freedom and lack the courage to stand up against misogyny,
racism, colonialism, and all forms of injustice. Her and the
other wo/men's testimony to the empty tomb is still heard
in the Easter liturgy and is the most frequent image in early
Christian art.

22. De Boer, *Mary Magdalene Cover Up*, 183.

Hippolytus of Rome who lived around 170–225 CE refers to the tradition of Mary's and the other wo/men's apostleship, which continued to be known in the Middle Ages, as follows:

> So that the women did not appear liars but bringers of the truth, Christ appeared to the [male] apostles and said to them: It is truly I who appeared to these women and who desired to send them to you as apostles.[23]

Several hundred years later, Gregory of Antioch who was a contemporary of Gregory the Great (d. 593) expresses the same understanding when he has Christ saying to the wo/men: "Be the first apostle to the apostles. So that Peter learns that I can choose even women as apostles."

According to Eastern Church tradition, when the male apostles departed from Jerusalem after Jesus's death and resurrection in order to preach the gospel to all the peoples and nations, Mary Magdalene also went with them. As apostle among the apostles she went beyond her native borders and went to preach in the center of the empire, Rome. She spoke everywhere to people about Christ and his teaching. When many did not believe that Jesus had been risen from the dead, she repeated to them what she had said to the apostles on the radiant morning of the Resurrection: "I have seen the Lord!" With this message she went according to tradition all around the Middle East and Italy.

When she came to Italy, Mary Magdalene is said to have visited Emperor Tiberius (14–37 CE) and proclaimed to him Christ's resurrection. According to this legend, she brought the emperor a red egg as a symbol of the resurrection, a symbol of new life with the words: "Christ is Risen!" Then she told the emperor that in his province of Judea the

23. Haskins, *Mary Magdalen*, 65n15.

unjustly condemned Jesus the Galilean, a holy man and miracle worker, powerful before God and all humanity, had been executed at the instigation of the Jewish high priests, and the sentence confirmed by the procurator appointed by Tiberius, Pontius Pilate. However, Jesus had risen from the dead. In order to explain the resurrection, Mary Magdalene picked up an egg from the dinner table. When the emperor said, that a person could no more raise from the dead than an egg turned red, the egg in her hand turned red.

I have invoked here the figure of Mary of Magdala as an example of wo/men's call to public leadership and at the same time as a woman who could also have said "me too." The image of her which I like best is found in the Episcopal Cathedral of San Francisco.[24] The modern artist has painted her as a wo/man of color holding in her hand an Easter egg as the symbol of new life.

This picture of Mary Magdalene with the egg in her hand expresses Mary of Magdala's significance as a witness to the fullness of life in the midst of injustice and death. This picture was painted by Robert Lentz OFM for Grace Cathedral in San Francisco to memorialize the election of Barbara Harris as the first woman ordained bishop in the Episcopal church. Mary of Magdala with the egg as a symbol of life in fullness calls not only women in the churches but also wo/men in public office to envision, defend, and make possible life in its fullness for all citizens of the globe.

TO CONCLUDE

A rabbinic story tells us that the distinguished Rabbi Akivah (ca 52–135 CE) renowned for his Torah interpretation, was visited by Moses. Sitting in the back of the classroom

24. Lentz. "St. Mary Magdalene—Roman by Br Robert Lentz OFM."

at the Akivah academy, Moses listened in wonder as Rabbi Akivah with great eloquence and exegetical skill explained the unfathomable mysteries of the Torah. When Moses asked, amazed, who had written such great things about which he had never heard, Rabbi Akivah answered: These are the words of the Torah given by G*d[25] to Moses.

What if Miryam had accompanied her brother Moses to Rabbi Akivah's academy and hearing him expound her story cried out in protest? Would she have been punished again with a skin disease for speaking out? Or what would Mary of Magdala who together with Jesus fostered a discipleship community of equals say when reading up on the many books written about her and Jesus? Would she not be puzzled and angry that scholars only credit Jesus and not also his companions with an egalitarian movement, a discipleship of equals, that they together had envisioned? Hearing that she was a whore and repentant sinner who was rescued by Jesus the great man, would she not laugh about such nonsense or break out in tears over such slander and silencing?

Last but not least: While the story of Miryam of Magdala, the apostle to the apostles was turned into the story of a great sinner and whore, the story of Miryam of Nazareth, the teenage unwed mother who in the Magnificat praised G*d as having "brought down the powerful and lifted up the lowly, who has filled the hungry with good things and sent the rich away"(Luke 1:52–53; full Magnificat is Luke 1:46–55) has been turned into the story of the sexually pure White Lady, the Queen of Heaven, the eternal Feminine of Romantic idealization and colonial power. All three Miryams or Mariams or Marys have left their deep cultural-political imprints not only in the imagination of three

25. I write G*d in this way to emphasize the inadequacy of language to express the divine.

"biblical" religions but also in public cultural and socio-political consciousness. Wo/men in public life have still to struggle with this threefold cultural imprint of sexual and mental abuse that is politically dangerous.

EPILOGUE

A WHOLE YEAR HAS passed between the writing of the introduction and the epilogue to this book. Joe Biden was elected as president and chose Kamala Harris, who was one of the presidential wo/men candidates, as his vice-president. Women have thus come very close to the presidency, but still are in a very feminine position of having secondary supportive status. This secondary status is instantiated every time the president speaks and the vice president stands in the background signaling a supportive role.

There are many reasons for this failure of the democratic cultural-political imagination. One of them, as I have suggested in this book, is the fact that we do not have a biblical imprint or cultural code for the presidency of wo/men. Such an imprint cannot simply be created at a desk. Rather, it must emerge from the public imagination of the people. I have attempted here to gesture toward this lacuna or unfilled space in the hope to start a discussion of the problem and a challenge to the popular imagination. Such a discussion is necessary as long as the religious Right invokes biblical imagery to support an anti-democratic mentality and vision.

BIBLIOGRAPHY

Aquino, Maria Pílar, et al., eds. *A Reader in Latina Feminist Theology.* Religion and Justice. Austin: University of Texas Press, 2002.

Armour, Ellen T. *Deconstruction, Feminist Theology and the Problem of Difference: Subverting the Race/Gender Divide.* Chicago: University of Chicago, 1999.

Attanasio, Cedar, et al. "Police: El Paso Shooting Suspect Said He Targeted Mexicans." *ABC News,* August 9, 2019. https://abcnews.go.com/US/wireStory/police-el-paso-shooting-suspect-targeted-mexicans-64886138.

Balch, David, and Carolyn Osiek, eds. *Early Christian Families in Context: An Interdisciplinary Dialogue.* Grand Rapids: Eerdmans, 2003.

Barber, William J. *The Third Reconstruction.* Boston: Beacon, 2016.

Barclay, John M.G. "The Family as the Bearer of Religion in Judaism and Early Christianity." In *Constructing Early Christian Families: Family as Social Reality and Metaphor,* edited by Halvor Moxnes, 66–80. London: Routledge, 1997.

Beach, Eleanor Ferris. *The Jezebel Letters Religion. and Politics in Ninth-Century Israel.* Minneapolis: Fortress, 2005.

Bendroth, Margaret Lamberts. *Fundamentalism and Gender. 1875 to the Present.* New Haven, CT: Yale University Press, 1993.

Berlin, Adele, and Marc Zvi Brettler, eds. *The Jewish Study Bible.* Oxford: Oxford University Press, 200.

Berlinerblau,. Jacques. *Thumpin' It: The Use and Abuse of the Bible in Today's Presidential Politics* Louisville: Westminster John Knox, 2008.

Blackmore, Erin. "Pope's New Nativity Scene Raises Awareness of Worldwide Refugee Crisis." Smithsonian Institution, December 14, 2016. https://www.smithsonianmag.com/smart-news/

popes-new-nativity-scene-raises-awareness-worldwide-refugee-crisis-180961415/.

Boyarin, Daniel. *The Jewish Gospels: The Story of the Jewish Christ.* New York: The New Press, 2012.

———. *A Radical Jew: Paul and the Politics of Identity.* Berkeley: University of California Press, 1994.

Bradley, Keith R. *Discovering the Roman Family: Studies in Roman Social History.* New York: Oxford University Press, 1991.

Briggs, Sheila. "Galatians." In *Searching the Scriptures: A Feminist Commentary Vol. II,* edited by Elisabeth Schüssler Fiorenza, 218–36. New York: Crossroad, 1994.

———. "Paul on Bondage and Freedom in Imperial Roman Society." In *Paul and Politics: Ekklesia, Israel and Imperium,* edited by Richard Horsley, 110–23. Harrisburg, PA: Trinity, 2000.

———. "Slavery and Gender." In *On the Cutting Edge: The Study of Women in Biblical Worlds,* edited by Jane Schaberg et al., 171–92. New York: Continuum, 2003.

Briggs, Sheila, et al., eds. *The Bible in the Public Square: Reading the Signs of the Times.* Minneapolis: Fortress, 2008.

Broner, Esther, and Naomi Nimrod. *The Telling.* 1st ed. San Francisco: Harper San Francisco, 1993.

Brown, Dan. *The Da Vinci Code.* New York: Doubleday, 2003.

Brown, Raymond E. *The Birth of the Messiah: A Commentary on the Infancy Narratives in the Gospels of Matthew and Luke.* Anchor Bible Reference Library. New York: Doubleday, 1993.

Brown, Robert McAfee. *Theology in a New Key: Responding to Liberation Themes.* 1st ed. Philadelphia: Westminster, 1978.

Bryson, Valerie. *Feminist Debates. Issues of Theory and Political Practice.* New York: New York University Press, 1999.

Burton, Tara Isabelle. "The Biblical Story the Christian Right Uses to Defend Trump." *Vox,* March 5, 2018. https://www.vox.com/identities/2018/3/5/16796892/trump-cyrus-christian-right-bible-cbn-evangelical-propaganda.

Bussman, Hadumond, and Renate Hof. *Geschlecherforschung/ Gender Studies in den Kultur und Sozialwissenschaften.* Stuttgart: Kröner 2005.

Callahan, Allen Dwight. *The Talking Book: African Americans and the Bible.* New Haven, CT: Yale University Press, 2006.

Canon, Katie. *Black Womanist Ethics.* AAR Academy Series 60. Atlanta: Scholars, 1988.

Chambers Jerald, Morgan. "Respectable Women: Exploring the Influence of the Jezebel Stereotype on Black Women's Sexual Well-Being." PhD diss., University of Michigan, 2018.

Champion, Craig B., ed. *Roman Imperialism. Readings and Sources* Malden, MA: Blackwell, 2004.

Chancey, Mark, et al., eds. *The Bible in the Public Square: Its Enduring Influence in American Life.* Atlanta: Society of Biblical Literature, 2014.

"Chaos Candidate: Is Trump a Modern-Day King Cyrus?" CBN. https://www1.cbn.com/content/chaos-candidate-trump-modern-day-king-cyrus.

Cohen, Shaye. *The Jewish Family in Antiquity.* Atlanta: Scholars, 1993.

Collins, Patricia Hill. "Controlling Images and Black Women's Oppression." In *Seeing Ourselves: Classic, Contemporary, and Cross-Cultural Readings in Sociology,* edited by John J. Macionis and Nijole V. Benokraitis, 266–73. New York: Pearson, 2009.

Coote, Mary P., and Robert B. *Power, Politics, and the Making of the Bible: An Introduction.* Minneapolis: Fortress, 1990.

Cox, Cheryl A. *Household Interests: Property, Marriage Strategies, and Family Dynamics in Ancient Athens.* Princeton: Princeton University Press, 1998.

Dabashi, Hamid. "Is Trump a King Cyrus or Queen Esther." *Al Jazeeera.* April 11, 2019. https://www.aljazeera.com/indepth/opinion/trump-king-cyrus-queen-esther-190411105108358.html.

De Boer, Esther. *The Mary Magdalene Cover Up.* London: T. & T. Clark, 2006.

De la Rosa, Jose. *Trump the US King Cyrus and the American Prayer.* Self-published, 2017.

Dekoven, Marianne, ed. *Feminist Locations. Lobal and Local Theory and Practice.* New Brunswick: Rutgers, 2001.

Dennis, Kate, dir. *The Handmaid's Tale.* Season 1, episode 8, "Jezebels."

DeYoung, Curtiss Paul, et al., eds. *The People's Bible* Minneapolis: Fortress, 2009.

Diamond, Sara. *Spiritual Warfare. The Politics of the Christian Right* Boston: South End, 1989.

Dijk-Hemmes, F. Van. "Sarai's Exile: A Gender Motivated Reading of Genesis 12:10–13:2." In *A Feminist Companion to Genesis*, edited by A. Brenner, 222–34. Sheffield: Sheffield Academic Press, 1997.

Dixon, Suzanne. *The Roman Family.* Baltimore: Johns Hopkins University Press, 1992.

Dutcher-Walls, Patricia. *Jezebel: Portraits of a Queen* Collegeville, PA: Liturgical, 2004.

Eck, Christine E. "Three Books, Three Stereotypes: Mothers and the Ghosts of Mammy, Jezebel and Sapphire in Contemporary African American Literature." *Criterion: A Journal of Literary Criticism* 11 (2018) 11–24.

ENCA. "Religious Abuse Addressed at Summit." November 30, 2018. https://www.youtube.com/watch?v=k3kosi88x0Y.

Fewell, Danna Noel. "Judges." In *Women's Bible Commentary*, edited by Carol A. Newsome and Sharon Ringe, 73–83. Louisville: Westminster John Knox, 1989.

Fowler, Robert M. *Let the Reader Understand: Reader Response Criticism and the Gospel of Mark.* Minneapolis: Fortress, 1991.

Frankel, Ellen. *The Five Books of Miriam: A Woman's Commentary on the Torah.* San Francisco: Harper San Francisco, 1998.

Frankfurter, David. "Revelation to John." In *The Jewish Annotated New Testament,* 471. Oxford: Oxford University Press, 2011.

"Fundalismen: Patriarchale Mogelpackung." *Beiträge zur feministischen Theorie und Praxis* 32 (1992).

Gafney, Wilda. "Hagar." Bible Odyssey. http://bibleodyssey.org/en/people/main-articles/hagar.

———. *Womanist Midrash: A Reintroduction to the Women of the Torah and the Throne.* Louisville: Presbyterian, 2017.

Gaines, Janet Howe. "How Bad Was Jezebel?" *Bible Review* 16 (2000) 12–23.

———. *Music in the Old Bones: Jezebel Through the Ages.* Carbondale: Southern Illinois University Press, 1999.

Gardner, Jane. *Family and Familia in Roman Law and Life.* Oxford: Oxford University Press, 1998.

Glancy, Jennifer. *Slavery in Early Christianity.* Oxford: Oxford University Press, 2006.

González, Karen. "Abraham Broke the Law, Crossing Borders and Trafficking his Wife: Why Do We Forgive Him So Much More Easily than Migrants Today?" *Christian Century* May 21, 2019. https://www.christiancentury.org/article/critical-essay/abraham-broke-law-crossing-borders-and-trafficking-his-wife.

Gordon, Taylor. "Black Women in the Media: Mammy, Jezebel, or Angry." *Atlanta Black Star,* March 4, 2013. https://atlantablackstar.com/2013/03/04/black-women-in-the-media-mammy-jezebel-or-angry/.

Graham, Ruth. "Why Evangelicals are Arguing Online about David and Bathsheba." *Slate,* October 10, 2019. https://slate.com/

human-interest/2019/10/bathsheba-david-rape-evangelical-abuse.html.

Grant, Robert M. *A Short History of Biblical Interpretation*. New York: Macmillan, 1963.

Grimké, Sarah, and Angelina Grimké. *On Slavery and Abolitionism: Essays and Letters*. Penguin Classics. New York: Penguin, 2014.

Hanson, Paul D. *A Political History of the Bible in America*. Louisville: Westminster John Knox, 2015.

Harris-Lacewell, Melissa Victoria. *Barbershops, Bibles, and BET: Everyday Talk and Black Political Thought*. Princeton: Princeton University Press, 2006.

Haskins, Susan. *Mary Magdalen: Truth and Myth*. London: Pimlico, 2005.

Hassan, Riffat. "Islamic Hagar and Her Family." In *Hagar, Sarah, and Their Children: Jewish, Christian, and Muslim Perspectives*, edited by Phyllis Trible and Letty M. Russel, 149–70. Louisville: Westminster John Knox, 2006.

Held Evans, Rachel. *Inspired: Slaying Giants, Walking on Water, and Loving the Bible Again*. Nashville: Nelson, 2018.

Hill Fletcher, Jeannine. *The Sin of White Supremacy: Christianity, Racism, and Religious Diversity in America*. Maryknoll, NY: Orbis, 2017.

Horowitz, Jason, et al. "Nine Killed in Shooting at Black Church in Charleston." *New York Times*, June 17, 2015. https://www.nytimes.com/2015/06/18/us/church-attacked-in-charleston-south-carolina.html.

Horsley, Richard A. *The Liberation of Christmas: The Infancy Narratives in Social Context*. New York: Crossroad, 1989.

Howland, Courtney W., ed. *Religious Fundamentalisms and the Human Rights of Women,* New York: Palgrave, 1999.

Iser, Wolfgang. *The Act of Reading: A Theory of Aesthetic Response* Baltimore: Johns Hopkins University Press, 1978.

Jefferson, Thomas. *The Jefferson Bible*. Radford, VA: Wilder, 2007.

Jeffries, Giovanna Miceli. *Feminine Feminists: Cultural Practices in Italy*. Minneapolis: University of Minnesota, 1994.

Jost, Renate. *Frauenmacht und Männerliebe. Egalitäre Utopien aus der Frühzeit Israels*. Stuttgart: Kohlhammer Verlag, 2006.

Kenski, Tikva Frymer. "Deborah." *My Jewish Learning*. https://www.myjewishlearning.com/article/deborah/.

Kittredge, Cynthia Briggs. *Community and Authority in Paul. The Rhetoric of Obedience in the Pauline Tradition*. Harrisburg, PA: Trinity, 1998.

Küng, Hans, and Jürgen Moltmann, eds. *Fundamentalism as an Ecumenical Challenge*. Concilium; London: SCM, 1992.

Lamb, David T. "David was a Rapist, Abraham was a Sex Trafficker." *Christianity Today*. October 22, 2015. https://www.christianitytoday.com/ct/2015/october-web-only/david-was-rapist-abraham-was-sex-trafficker.html.

Lassen, Eva-Marie. "The Roman Family: Ideal and Metaphor." In *Constructing Early Christian Families: Family as Social Reality and Metaphor*, edited by Halvor Moxnes, 103–20. London: Routledge, 1997.

Lentz, Br. Robert, OFM. "St. Mary Magdalene—Roman by Br Robert Lentz OFM." Fine Art America, n.d. https://fineartamerica.com/featured/st-mary-magdalene-rlmam-br-robert-lentz-ofm.html.

Lernoux, Penny. *Cry of the People*. New York: Penguin, 1982.

———. *In Banks We Trust*. New York: Penguin, 1986.

———. *People of God. The Struggle for World Catholicism*. New York: Penguin, 1989.

Lomax, Tamura. *Jezebel Unhinged. Loosing the Black Female Body in Religion and Culture*. Durham: Duke University Press, 2018.

Martin, Dale B. "The Construction of the Ancient Family: Methodological Considerations." *Journal of Roman Studies* 86 (1996) 40–60.

Mason, Carol. *Killing for Life: The Apocalyptic Narrative of Pro-Life Politics*. Ithaca, NY: Cornell University Press, 2002.

Mason, Jeff, and Susan Cornwell. "Trump Defiant as Lawmakers Blast his 'Racist' Attacks on Four Congresswomen." *Reuters*, July 14, 2019. https://www.reuters.com/article/us-usa-trump-democrats/trump-defiant-as-lawmakers-blast-his-racist-attacks-on-four-congresswomen-idUSKCN1U90H7.

Meyers, Carol. "Miriam, Music, and Miracles." In *Mariam, the Magdalen and the Mother,* edited by Deirdre Good, 27–48. Bloomimgton: Indiana University Press, 2005.

Miller, John Maxwell, and John Hayes. *A History of Ancient Israel and Judah*. Philadelphia: Westminster, 1986.

Moller Okin, Susan. *Justice, Gender, and the Family*. New York: Basic, 1989.

———. *Women in Western Political Thought*. Princeton: Princeton University Press, 1979.

Moss, Candida. "Biblical Sites, Ancient Wonders, the Last 'Garden of Eden': Here's What Trump Just Threatened to Bomb in Iran." *The Daily Beast,* January 6, 2020. https://www.thedailybeast.com/

here-are-the-biblical-wonders-trump-just-threatened-to-bomb-in-iran.

Nagl-Docekal, Herta. *Feminist Philosophy*. Boulder, CO: Westview, 2004.

Nash, Robert Scott. "Heuristic Haustafeln: Domestic Codes as Entrance to the Social World of Early Christianity: The Case of Colossians." In *Religious Writings and Religious Systems: Systemic Analysis of Holy Books in Christianity, Islam, Buddhism, Greco-Roman Religions, Ancient Israel, and Judaism*, edited by Jacob Neusner et al., 25–50. Atlanta: Scholars, 1989.

New York Times Editorial Team. "The Democrats' Best Choice for President." *New York Times*, January 19, 2020. https://www.nytimes.com/interactive/2020/01/19/opinion/amy-klobuchar-elizabeth-warren-nytimes-endorsement.html.

Nicolaou, Elena, and Courtney E. Smith. "A #MeToo Timeline To Show How Far We've Come—& How Far We Need To Go." Refinery29, October 5, 2019. https://www.refinery29.com/en-us/2018/10/212801/me-too-movement-history-timeline-year-weinstein.

O'Donnell, Jonathon. "The Body Politic(s) of the Jezebel Spirit." *Religion and Gender* 7 (2017) 240–55.

Ophoff, Rachel. "Debunking the Trump-Cyrus Prophecy." *Red Letter Christians*, November 5, 2019. https://www.redletterchristians.org/debunking-the-trump-cyrus-prophecy/.

Osiek, Carolyn, and Margaret Y. MacDonald. *A Woman's Place: House Churches in Early Christianity*. Minneapolis: Fortress, 2006.

Pilgrim, David. "The Jezebel Stereotype." Jim Crow Museum of Racist Memorabilia. https://www.ferris.edu/HTMLS/news/jimcrow/jezebel/index.htm.

Pippin, Tina. "Jezebel Revamped." In *Apocalyptic Bodies: The Biblical End of the World in Text and Image*, 32–41. New York: Routledge, 1999.

Radl, Shirley Rogers. *The Invisible Woman. Target of the Religious New Right*. New York: Dell, 1981.

Rapaille, Clotaire. *The Culture Code: An Ingenious Way to Understand Why People Around the World Live and Buy as They Do*. New York: Crown Business, 2006.

Rapp, Ursula *Mirjam. Eine feministisch-rhetorische Lektüre der Mirjamtexte in der hebräischen Bibel*. Berlin and New York: de Gruyter, 2002.

Rawson, Beryl. "Children as Cultural Symbols: Imperial Ideology in the 2nd Century." In *Childhood, Class, and Kin in the Roman*

World, edited by Suzanne Dixon, 37–58. London: Routledge, 2001.

———. *Marriage, Family and Divorce in Ancient Rome.* Oxford: Oxford University Press, 1996.

Reich, Robert B. *The Work of Nations.* New York: Vintage, 1992.

Reilly, Frank. "Jane Schaberg, Raymond E. Brown, and the Problem of the Illegitimacy of Jesus." *Journal of Feminist Studies in Religion* 21 (2005) 57–80.

"Report of the Task Force on Circumcision." *Pediatrics* 84 (1989) 388–91.

Robertson, Campbell, et al. "11 Killed in Synagogue Massacre; Suspect Charged With 29 Counts." *New York Times,* October 27, 2018. https://www.nytimes.com/2018/10/27/us/active-shooter-pittsburgh-synagogue-shooting.html.

Saller, Richard. "Corporal Punishment, Authority, and Obedience in the Roman Household." In *Marriage, Divorce, and Children in Ancient Rome*, edited by Beryl Rawson, 144–65. Canberra: Humanities Research Center, 1991.

———. "Pater Familias, Mater Familias, and the Gendered Semantics of a Roman Household." *CP* 94 (1999) 182–97.

———. *Patriarchy, Property, and Death in the Roman Family.* Cambridge: Cambridge University Press, 1994.

———. "Women, Slaves, and the Economy of the Roman Household." In *Early Christian Families in Context: an Interdisciplinary Dialogue,* edited by David Balch and Carolyn Osiek, 185–206. Grand Rapids: Eerdmans, 2003.

Salo, Jackie. "Church under Fire for Nativity Scene Depicting Jesus, Mary and Joseph as Caged Refugees." *New York Post*, December 9, 2019. https://nypost.com/2019/12/09/church-under-fire-for-nativity-scene-depicting-jesus-mary-and-joseph-as-caged-refugees/.

Sandoval, Chela. *Methodology of the Oppressed.* Minneapolis: University of Minnesota Press, 2000.

Schaberg, Jane. "Feminist Interpretations of the Infancy Narrative of Matthew." *Journal of Feminist Studies in Religion* 13 (1997) 35–62.

———. *The Illegitimacy of Jesus: A Feminist Theological Interpretation of the Infancy Narratives.* San Francisco: Harper & Row, 1987.

Schneider, Tammi J. *Sarah, Mother of Nations.* New York; Continuum, 2004.

Scholz, Susann. *The Bible as Political Artifact: On the Feminist Study of the Hebrew Bible*. Minneapolis: Fortress, 2017.

——. *Biblical Studies Alternatively: An Introductory Reader* New York: Prentice Hall, 2003.

Schüssler Fiorenza, Elisabeth. *The Book of Revelation: Justice and Judgement.* 2nd ed. Minneapolis: Fortress, 1998.

——. *But She Said: Feminist Practices of Biblical Interpretation.* Boston: Beacon, 1992.

——. *Democratizing Biblical Studies: Toward an Emancipatory Educational Space.* Louisville: Westminster John Knox, 2009.

——. *Discipleship of Equals: A Critical Feminist Ekklēsia-Logy of Liberation.* New York: Crossroad, 1993.

——. *In Memory of Her: A Feminist Theological Reconstruction of Christian Origins.* Tenth Anniversary Edition. New York: Crossroad, 1994.

——. *Jesus: Miriam's Child, Sophia's Prophet: Critical Issues in Feminist Christology.* New York: Continuum, 1994.

——. *Jesus and the Politics of Interpretation.* New York: Continuum, 2000.

——. *Sharing Her Word: Feminist Biblical Interpretation in Context.* Boston: Beacon, 1998.

——. *Wisdom Ways: Introducing Feminist Biblical Interpretation* Maryknoll, NY: Orbis, 2001.

——. "The Words of Prophecy: Reading the Apocalypse Theologically." In *Studies in the Book of Revelation,* edited by Steve Moyise, 1–20. Edinburgh: T. & T. Clark, 2001.

Schüssler Fiorenza, Elisabeth, and Laura Nasrallah, eds. *Prejudice and Christian Beginnings: Investigating Race, Gender, and Ethnicity in Early Christian Studies.* Minneapolis: Fortress, 2009.

Shanley, Mary Lyndon, and Caroline Pateman, eds. *Feminist Interpretations and Political Theory.* University Park: Penn State University Press, 1991.

Smith, Joan. "The Creation of the World We Know: The World-Economy and the Re-creation of Gendered Identities." In *Identity Politics and Women. Cultural Reassertions and Feminisms in International Perspective,* edited by Valentine M. Moghadam, 27–41. Boulder, CO: Westview, 1994.

Standhartinger, Angela. "The Origin and Intention of the Household Code in the Letter to the Colossians." *JSNT* 79 (2000) 117–30.

Syme, Ronald. *The Roman Revolution.* Oxford: Oxford University Press, 1939.

Tannen, Deborah. "The Self-Fulfilling Prophecy of Disliking Hillary Clinton." *Time,* March 15, 2016. https://time.com/4258976/disliking-hillary-clinton/.

Tracy, David, and Robert M. Grant. *A Short History of Biblical Interpretation*. Minneapolis: Fortress, 2009.

Trible, Phyllis. "Bringing Miriam out of the Shadows." *Bible Review* 5 (1989) 14–25.

Trible, Phyllis, and Letty M. Russell, eds. *Hagar, Sarah, and Their Children: Jewish, Christian and Muslim Perspectives*. Louisville: Westminster John Knox, 2006.

Walby, Sylvia. *Patriarchy at Work*. Minneapolis: University of Minnesota, 1986.

Werline, Frances, and Rodney A. Flannery, eds. *The Bible in Political Debate: What Does it Really Say?* Edinburgh: T. & T. Clark, 2016.

West, Darrell M. "It's Time to Abolish the Electoral College." Brookings Institution. https://www.brookings.edu/wp-content/uploads/2019/10/Big-Ideas_West_Electoral-College.pdf.

Williams, Delores. "Hagar in African American Biblical Appropriation." In *Hagar, Sarah, and Their Children: Jewish, Christian, and Muslim Perspectives*, edited by Phyllis Trible and Letty M. Russell, 171–84. Louisville: Westminster John Knox, 2006.

Worthington, Frances. "Hagar and Ishmael in the Wilderness." *Baha'i Teachings*, May 4, 2016. https://bahaiteachings.org/abraham-hagar-ishmael-in-wilderness/.

Julia 206 070
        3975

we
can
put
her
up

Made in the USA
Middletown, DE
21 May 2022

f

fatigue

In *Wo/men, Scripture, and Politics*, Elisabeth Schüssler Fiorenza, brings to bear years of trailblazing scholarship of feminist thought and hermeneutics onto the current political and cultural landscape. In this book, she seeks to articulate and use biblical interpretation as intervention into the failure of the democratic cultural-political imagination. Although such an intervention is often taboo for supposedly neutral academic scholarship, Schüssler Fiorenza argues that it is politically necessary because political argument today so often utilizes biblical rhetoric in the public square. The biblical-political analysis and suggestions of this book are developed in four chapters, each focusing on the role of the Bible in struggles over women's leadership in the present, touching on the cultural "double bind" of women in politics, sexual abuse, power, and the #MeToo movement. Schüssler Fiorenza's insights and arguments not only lead to the development of reimagined cultural biblical imprints of women in the political arena, but they also encourage her readers to add their own biblical examples to inspire them in their struggle for a biblical vision of "women in the public square." This is an insightful, challenging book written for our time by someone who has always seemed to be ahead of hers.

> "As more and more women move into politics, progressive people ignore religious texts at their peril. Scriptural narratives shape election outcomes; conservative evangelical theologies, both Catholic and Protestant, delivered the votes for a presidential demagogue. Dr. Schüssler Fiorenza's analysis exposes the dangers of patriarchal biblical studies and illuminates what feminist, theo-political-savvy faith traditions need to do to avoid a repeat performance. Her work creates a safer and more just world, especially for women and children."
>
> —MARY E. HUNT, Codirector, Women's Alliance for Theology, Ethics and Ritual (WATER)

Elisabeth Schüssler Fiorenza, the Krister Stendahl Professor of Divinity at Harvard Divinity School, has been one of the leading scholars of feminist theology and interpretation for over three decades. She is author of many important and influential works, among them *In Memory of Her: A Feminist Theological Reconstruction of Christian Origins* (1983) and *Changing Horizons: Explorations in Feminist Interpretation* (2013). Schüssler Fiorenza is founding co-editor of the *Journal of Feminist Studies in Religion* and past president of the Society of Biblical Literature.

COVER DESIGN: Savanah N. Landerholm
www.wipfandstock.com

Cascade Books
An Imprint of WIPF and STOCK Publishers

ISBN 978-1-4982-3532-7

9 781498 235327